PRIDE OF THE SOUTH
CONFEDERATE LEADERS OF THE CIVIL WAR

American History Archives™

Pride of the South
Confederate Leaders of the Civil War

4 5 6 / 09 08 07 06
ISBN 1-58159-242-6

The History Channel Club
c/o North American Membership Group
12301 Whitewater Drive
Minnetonka, MN 55343
www.thehistorychannelclub.com

Published by North American Membership Group under license from Osprey
Publishing Ltd.

Previously published as Elite 88: *American Civil War Commanders (2)
Confederate Leaders in the East* and Elite 94: *American Civil War Commanders
(4) Confederate Leaders in the West* by Osprey Publishing, Midland House,
West Way, Botley, Oxford OX2 0PH, United Kingdom

© 2005 Osprey Publishing Ltd.   OSPREY
PUBLISHING

Editor: Martin Windrow
Design: Alan Hamp
Index by Glyn Sutcliffe
Originated by Magnet Harlequin and The Electronic Page Company, UK
Printed in China through World Print Ltd.

FRONT COVER
Robert E. Lee. (NARA)

Author's Note

It should be acknowledged that, for reasons of space, there are
only the most basic notes on the careers of some of the most
important figures, The author has tried to give a flavor of their
characters and appearance, but for any seriously detailed analysis
of their command service the reader is recommended to the
existing biographies.

While American conventions of spelling and punctuation have been
used throughout the text, readers may notice historical variations in
passages directly quoted from 19th century sources.

All monochrome illustrations in Part I are from the collection of the
Military Images magazine.

**Author PHILIP KATCHER was born in Los Angeles, California,
to parents involved in the film industry. He was educated at
the University of Maryland and served in the
US Army in Vietnam. He has also been an active participant
in living history activities, especially in the 18th and
19th century periods. He has written a number of books
on various periods of US military history and presently is
editor/publisher of *Military Images Magazine*.**

**Illustrator RICHARD HOOK was born in 1938 and trained at
Reigate College of Art. After national service with 1st Bn,
Queen's Royal Regiment he became art editor of the much-
praised magazine *Finding Out* during the 1960s. He has
worked as a freelance illustrator ever since, earning an
international reputation particularly for his deep knowledge
of Native American material culture; and has illustrated more
than 30 Osprey titles. Richard is married and lives in Sussex.**

PRIDE OF THE SOUTH
Confederate Leaders of the Civil War

CONTENTS

INTRODUCTION

It was, altogether and all told, one of the most magnificent armies ever created. Not in terms of sheer numbers, fancy equipment, or training and discipline. But for bravery, sheer fighting ability and dogged willpower, the world has never seen an army like that of the Confederate States of America.

Of course, the rank-and-file foot soldiers, artillery men and cavalry did most of the fighting. But superb leadership was the key behind the success that the Confederate forces achieved for so long against an opponent with more men and more materiel.

Here are the stories of those smart, courageous, feisty, determined—and sometimes quirky—Confederate leaders.

In Part 1 - Confederate Leaders in the East, you'll discover the details behind the careers, personalities and appearance of 25 commanders who made their names mainly with the Army of Northern Virginia in the Eastern theater of war. Their stories are fascinating—wonderful bites of American History.

In Part 2 - Confederate Leaders in the West, you'll find the same kind of detail and historical facts, this time on the 24 generals of the Army of Tennessee and other key Confederate commanders in the West. They faced the Union's best generals and were always outnumbered. But they fought well.

America's history—and in particular the details about the Civil War—is about much more than just dates and places. It's also about the people who made things happen. Here's a chance to discover essential details behind the *Pride of the South—Confederate Leaders of the Civil War.*

OPPOSITE **Jefferson Davis (1808–89), as President of the Confederate States of America, was commander-in-chief of the Confederate forces by the provisions of the Confederate Constitution. A former West Point graduate who had served in several frontier campaigns, this Mississippian later resigned his commission in favor of a political career, but returned to the colors as commander of a volunteer regiment in the Mexican War, distinguishing himself at Buena Vista. This episode, and his time as Secretary of War under President Pierce in 1853–57, gave him considerable confidence in his own military abilities, but he was essentially an administrator. As a workaholic who found it hard to delegate, he dominated several successive nominal heads of the Confederate War Department, and reserved to himself the right to appoint and promote generals. Davis was imprisoned for two years after the war, but was never brought to trial for treason, and was included in the amnesty of 1872.**

PART 1

CONFEDERATE LEADERS IN THE EAST

INTRODUCTION

I N ALL, 425 MEN RECEIVED THE RANK OF GENERAL from the Congress of the Confederate States of America. Originally there was only one general grade rank, that of brigadier-general; but quite soon after the Confederate Army's formation full generals were commissioned, while the rank of major-general was created for divisional commanders. When corps were adopted, the rank of lieutenant-general was created for that command.

Most Confederate generals were professional soldiers who had been educated at a military school and had seen active military service. The highest ranks were largely filled by graduates of the United States Military Academy at West Point, New York, although the Virginia Military Institute also provided the Confederacy with a number of general officers. None had commanded so much as a brigade in the pre-war US Army, so essentially each of them had to learn the practise of senior command "on the job."

The regulation general's uniform included a double-breasted gray frock coat with buff facings – collar, pointed cuffs, and edging. There were two rows of eight front buttons placed in pairs. Four lines of gold lace formed an Austrian knot on each sleeve; collar insignia were in the form of three gold stars within a wreath, the center one larger. Trousers were dark blue with gold parallel stripes down each outside seam; and a buff waist sash was to be worn over the coat. Officially the headgear was a *chapeau bras* or cocked bicorn hat reminiscent of the Napoleonic era, but a dark blue French-style kepi trimmed with four parallel gold cords was authorized for field use.

In practice very few generals wore strictly regulation uniforms. The gray fabrics used for the coat varied from light or dark ash-gray to blue-gray shades. Facings – where present at all – were often of a buff so light as to appear virtually white. Many had evenly spaced buttons, while major-generals often wore two rows of nine buttons set in threes. Starting with Robert E.Lee, a number of senior generals wore on their collars three stars of the same size – actually a colonel's regulation rank badge; indeed, so many did so that this must have been a generally accepted insignia.

Staffs

Each general was authorized a staff to assist him in exercising command. These varied in size and scope. Lee's staff was remarkably small to run an entire army. Moxley Sorrel, at first an officer on Longstreet's staff and later a general in his own right, later put down his impressions of Lee's staff:

"His staff was small and efficient. I suppose that at this date there are some hundreds of men in the South who call themselves members of Lee's staff, and so they were if teamsters, sentry men, detailed quarter-masters (commissary men), couriers and orderlies, and all the rest of the following of general headquarters of a great army are to be so considered. But by staff we usually confine our-selves to those responsible officers immediately about a general, and Lee had selected carefully. Four majors (afterwards lieutenant-colonels and colonels) did the principal work." These were aides de camps and adjutants, while the army staff also included such individuals as the chief of artillery, chief commissary, chief ordnance officer, and chief surgeon.

Not only were these too few officers to adequately perform the staff work for such a large force; but the men picked usually had civilian backgrounds – they were often, in fact, relatives of the general, with little knowledge and inadequate training for their jobs. E.Porter Alexander thought that this was one cause of the piecemeal attacks made by the army in the Wilderness: "I think this is but one more illustration of one of the inherent weaknesses of our army in its lack of an abundance of trained & professional soldiers in the staff corps to make constant studies of all matters of detail."

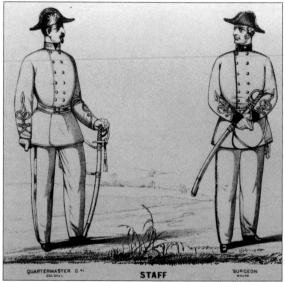

Pickett's divisional staff at Gettysburg included three aides, a chief of the division pioneer corps, a provost marshal, an assistant adjutant & inspector general and an assistant adjutant general, a commissary of subsistence, a chief ordnance officer, a chief surgeon, a quartermaster, and a paymaster. Enlisted men filled the posts of division postmaster, blacksmith, pioneers, headquarters guards, provost guards, clerks, teamsters, ordnance train guards, and commissary and commissary train workers.

Brigade staffs were even smaller, with most generals having simply an aide-de-camp, an assistant adjutant general, a quartermaster, a commissary of subsistence, an ordnance officer, and a couple of couriers, clerks, and wagoners. Some brigade staffs also included post-masters, surgeons, provost marshals, and assistant inspector generals.

An official Confederate Army
print showing the regulation
general's and staff officer's
dress. The general officer is
on the left, with a colonel
acting as adjutant general
in the center and a colonel
of engineers on the right.

An official Confederate
Army print of two staff
officers: a colonel acting
as quartermaster general
on the left, and a surgeon
ranking as a major, with
black facings.

BIOGRAPHIES: EAST

ALEXANDER, Edward Porter (1835–1910)

Edward Porter Alexander (**see Plate F3**) was born in Washington, Georgia, on 26 May 1835, to a wealthy plantation family. Privately tutored, he entered the US Military Academy and was graduated third in the class of 1857. His intelligence being obvious to his superiors, he was assigned to duty immediately after graduation as an instructor at West Point, while being commissioned into the Corps of Engineers. Interrupting his teaching to serve on the Mormon Expedition in 1857, he returned to the Academy in 1858 and was promoted to a full second lieutenant's rank. The next year he assisted US Army Surgeon Albert J.Myer in developing a system of signals that used flags during the day and torches at night. In 1860 he was sent to Fort Steilacoom, Washington Territory.

When the Civil War broke out Alexander went to San Francisco, resigned from the US Army, and traveled to Richmond. He was immediately commissioned a captain of engineers in the Confederate Army, and was sent to P.G.T.Beauregard's Army of the Potomac near Manassas Junction to set up a signal organization. From one of the observation towers he had built on the ground around that army he provided early information on the Union flank movement during First Manassas (Bull Run). This earned him praise; he was offered the position of the army's chief signal officer, but preferred a field command. He transferred into the artillery and was assigned the position of chief ordnance officer – while continuing to serve as chief signal officer – of Beauregard's army, which eventually became the Army of Northern Virginia under Robert E.Lee. Alexander was promoted to major of artillery on 18 April 1862, and to lieutenant-colonel of artillery 60 days later.

Moxley Sorrel told a story about Alexander: "In the early days of the war I one day met him, mounted as usual on a very sorry, doubtful looking beast, with a pair of enormous holsters on his saddle-horn. 'And what have you there, Alexander?' I asked, thinking possibly of some good edibles. 'These,' he said, and drew out his long telescope for reconnaissance – a very powerful glass – and from the other an enormous old-fashioned horse-pistol of immense calibre, some tiny cubes of lead, cut from bullets, and a pinch or two of gunpowder. 'Quail,' he said, 'are eating up this country and I like them. This old pistol gives me many a mess of birds.'"

He served with distinction at Fredericksburg (13 December 1862); and when the artillery was reorganized into battalions in the winter of 1862–63 Alexander was named a colonel (3 March 1863) and given one of them to command. At Chancellorsville (May 1863) his handling of the artillery allowed the two Confederate flanks to unite; and at Gettysburg (3 July 1863) his guns preceded Pickett's Charge – indeed, Longstreet even had Alexander give Pickett the exact word when to commence the charge, so well did the corps commander trust the young artilleryman.

Alexander functioned as corps chief of artillery when Longstreet's corps went to Chickamauga and Knoxville. Seeing his work, the Army of Tennessee's commander requested that Col. Alexander be promoted to brigadier-general and assigned as chief of that army's artillery. Lee, however, strongly objected: Jefferson Davis noted that Alexander was "one of the very few whom Gen. Lee would not give to anybody." Instead Alexander was commissioned a brigadier-general and named chief of artillery in I Corps of the Army of Northern Virginia on 19 March 1864. He designed many of the defensive works around Petersburg during that siege, retreating to Appomattox where his guns formed the Army of Northern Virginia's last defensive lines.

After the war Alexander held a number of positions. He taught at the University of South Carolina while investing in cottonseed production. Finally he entered the railroad business, where his record earned him the nickname of "the young Napoleon of the Railways." He retired in 1892, but was called into service as arbitrator of a boundary dispute between Nicaragua and Costa Rica, a job that lasted from 1897 to 1902. He returned home and died on 28 April 1910, in Savannah. He was buried in the City Cemetery in Augusta, Georgia.

Richard Heron Anderson was photographed in a plain gray frock coat with buttons arranged in threes, which indicated a major-general in the US Army. See Plate H2. (National Archives)

ANDERSON, Richard Heron (1821–79)

Richard Heron Anderson (see Plate H2) was born near Statesburg, South Carolina, on 7 October 1821. Graduating 40th in the class of 1842 from West Point, he was commissioned into the dragoons, serving in the Mexican, Mormon, and Comanche Wars.

At the outbreak of the Civil War he resigned his commission and, on 16 March 1861, was commissioned a regular Confederate Army major of cavalry and appointed colonel of the 1st South Carolina Infantry Regiment, serving during the bombardment of Fort Sumter. He was promoted to brigadier-general on 18 July 1861, and assigned to the Army of Pensacola. He was wounded in the left arm during the Santa Rosa Raid. Charged with being drunk while under fire, he was transferred to the Army of Northern Virginia on 31 January 1861 before the court martial could meet.

Commanding a brigade on the Peninsula in spring 1862, he assumed command of Longstreet's division as senior brigadier at several points, and was named a major-general on 14 July 1861. He fought well at Second Manassas (August 1862), but a thigh wound sidelined him until mid-November that year, when he returned to command. On 7 May 1864, on Longstreet's being wounded, Anderson was given command of I Corps, since he had previously served in that command and was the best known to its men of all available major-generals thought capable of the position. He was given the temporary rank of lieutenant-general from 31 May.

He fought well at Spotsylvania, but the offensive he ordered at Cold Harbor failed due to unco-ordinated attacks. When Longstreet resumed command, Anderson was given command of P.G.T.Beauregard's old corps, the so-called IV Corps – amounting to little more than a single division – near Petersburg. There he fought at Gravelly Run and White Oak Road, retreating afterwards until his corps was essentially destroyed at Sailor's Creek. With nothing left for him to command, Lee relieved him from duty on 8 April 1865, but by that time Anderson considered the war wholly lost regardless of anything the Confederates could do.

E.Porter Alexander would write of him that "Gen. Dick Anderson was as pleasant a commander to serve under as could be wished, & was a sturdy & reliable fighter." At the same time, a civilian acquaintance and fellow South Carolinian, Mary Chestnut, described him as "the most silent and discreet of men." According to Moxley Sorrel, "His courage was of the highest order, but he was indolent. His capacity and intelligence excellent, but it was hard to get him to use them. Withal, of a nature so true and lovable that it goes against me to criticize him … Longstreet knew him well, and could get a good deal out of him, more than any one else." Sorrel added that the "chivalrous, deliberate" Anderson "was a very brave man, but of a rather inert, indolent manner for commanding troops in the field, and by no means pushing or aggressive … He seemed to leave the corps much to his staff … I sometimes found myself sleeping in the same tent with him. He had a way on waking of sitting on his bed and proceeding to mend and patch his belongings out of a well-filled sailor's 'necessaire' he always carried – clothing, hats, boots, bridles, saddles, everything came handy to him. He caught me once watching this work, and said, smiling: 'You are wondering, I see; so did my wife when first married. She thought she would do the mending, but I told her I ought to have a little recreation occasionally."

Anderson was not very ambitious. Later in the war in West Virginia staff officer Francis Dawson was present when his command joined that of Jubal Early: "General Anderson ranked General Early, but did not wish to take command of his troops," Dawson noticed, "as he would necessarily have done when the two commands operated together."

The post-war years were unkind, and Anderson lived in near poverty, dying on 26 June 1879. He is buried in Beauford, South Carolina.

ARMISTEAD, Lewis Addison (1817–63)

Lewis Addison Armistead (see Plate E3) was born in New Bern, North Carolina, on 18 February 1817. After early schooling he entered West Point in 1834; but his Academy career came to an end after only two years when he broke a plate over the head of fellow cadet Jubal Early.

Despite this experience, Armistead still desired a military career and managed to win a direct commission in the US Army in 1839. During his service fellow officer John Magruder nicknamed Armistead "Lo," short for Lothario, and the nickname followed him throughout the rest of his life. The Mexican War found Armistead a lieutenant in the 6th US Infantry. With his regiment he saw action in the drive to Mexico City, although he missed the capture of the city as he was still recovering from a wound received in the assault on Chapultepec. He was twice breveted for bravery during the war, finishing it as a first lieutenant. He was promoted to captain, but resigned that rank on 25 May 1861 when the Civil War broke out.

Armistead was commissioned colonel of the 57th Virginia Infantry on 25 September 1861. After service that year in western Virginia and North Carolina, the regiment was sent to the defense of Richmond. He was named a brigadier-general on 1 April 1862, and given a brigade to command. During the fighting of 1 June on the Peninsula his commander, D.H.Hill, reported that Armistead's brigade "fled early in the action, with the exception of a few heroic companies, with which that gallant officer [Armistead] maintained his ground against an entire Brigade." As a result of the quality of his leadership, his brigade was given the job of leading the forlorn assault on Malvern Hill. Attacking in the teeth of tremendous artillery fire, the brigade lost 400 men in this action. One of Armistead's men felt that he was a "gallant, kind and urbane old veteran," although he was also known as a strict disciplinarian.

Armistead's brigade served in the reserve at Second Manassas in August 1862. In the Maryland campaign that followed Armistead was given the job of provost marshal with the task of sending forward the many Army of Northern Virginia stragglers. However, he returned to front-line duty at Sharpsburg (Antietam) the following month, when his brigade, attached to McLaws' division, attacked the Federals in the West Woods. There Armistead was wounded and had to give up command to one of his colonels. After he recovered his brigade was assigned to George Pickett's new division. It was held in reserve at Fredericksburg (13 December 1862), and missed Chancellorsville the following May when Pickett's division was sent to south-eastern Virginia that spring.

On the third day of the battle of Gettysburg (3 July 1863), Pickett's division was named a lead element in the assault on the Union center on Cemetery Ridge. The troops facing them were commanded by Winfield Scott Hancock, one of Armistead's closest friends in the pre-war US Army. Pickett placed his three brigades in two lines, two in the lead and Armistead's behind them. After an artillery barrage appeared to drive off the Union artillery from the objective, the infantry was ordered forward. Armistead himself, instead of remaining in the rear for better command control, strode at the head of his line, at some point during the advance sticking his black broad-brimmed hat on the point of his sword. As the march continued under Union fire that tore holes in the Confederate ranks, some noticed that the hat began to slip down the sword, so it eventually rested on the hilt. Crossing the Emmitsburg road, many men fell out of the ranks and ducked down there for cover from the fire that was destroying the division. Finally the remainder reached the wall marking the Federal front line. Armistead shouted, "Boys, give them the cold steel!

Who will follow me?" He rushed through the mass of fighting men, placed his hand on a Federal cannon barrel, and was shot three times, in the leg, arm, and chest.

Notoriously, the attack failed with huge loss. Armistead was taken from the field; it is said that he asked for Hancock, but the Union general had himself been carried off seriously wounded. Although two of Armistead's wounds were minor, the third was apparently missed by Federal surgeons, and he died on 5 July. He was buried on the site at the George Spangler farm, but several weeks later his body was disinterred and embalmed. The Philadelphia doctor who had this done hoped for compensation for such an act by Armistead's friends, but none was forthcoming, and Armistead was eventually reburied in St Paul's Cemetery in Baltimore.

EARLY, Jubal Anderson (1816–94)

Jubal Early **(see Plate G2)** was born in Virginia on 3 November 1816. Graduating 18th in the West Point class of 1837, he resigned after service in Florida to study law. After passing the bar he practiced in Rocky Mount, Virginia, which he represented in the Virginia House of Delegates. He was appointed the commonwealth's attorney, and also served as a major of Virginia Volunteers during the Mexican War (1846–48).

Although against secession, Early remained loyal to his native state when the Civil War began, and was named colonel of the 24th Virginia Infantry. Following his good work in July 1861 at First Manassas (Bull Run), he was appointed a brigadier-general on 21 July; and was promoted to major-general from 17 January 1863.

"General Early was a bachelor, with a pungent style of commenting on things he did not like," John B.Gordon wrote; "but he had a kind heart ..."

He was well respected by his superiors. Stonewall Jackson once demanded to know why he saw so many stragglers at the rear of Early's division; Early sent a message back "informing him that he saw so many stragglers in rear of my Division to-day, probably because he rode in the rear of my Division." Any other officer would have found himself under arrest for such a reply – but Jackson merely laughed.

With his subordinates he was less popular. Staff officer Henry Kyd Douglas wrote that "he received with impatience and never acted upon, either advice or suggestions from his subordinates. Arbitrary, cynical, with strong prejudices, he was personally disagreeable; he made few admirers or friends either by his manners or his habits ... If he had a tender feeling, he endeavored to conceal it and acted as though he would be ashamed to be detected in doing a kindness ..."

According to staff officer Moxley Sorrel, "Intellectually he was perhaps the peer of the best for strategic combinations, but he lacked ability to handle troops effectively in the field; that is, he was deficient in tactical skill. His irritable disposition and biting tongue made him anything but popular, but he was a very brave and able commander."

Jubal Early appears here in a regulation general's coat with buff standing collar and his buttons arranged in threes.

In the field Jubal Early wore a gray "sack coat" style with a turned-down collar, the insignia embroidered on a buff oval and sewn to the top of the collar – see plate G2.

Gordon felt that Early "was an able strategist and one of the coolest and most imperturbable of men under fire and in extremity." Despite this, "he lacked what I shall term official courage, or what is known as the courage of one's convictions … [and had an] indisposition to act upon suggestions submitted by subordinates and his distrust of the accuracy by scouts …"

"Quick to decide and almost inflexible in decision, with a boldness to attack that approached rashness and a tenacity in resisting desperation, he was yet on the field of battle not equal to his own intellect or decision," staff officer Douglas agreed, noting that, "He moved slowly from point to point …"

Despite these flaws he was promoted to lieutenant-general from 31 May 1864. Later James Longstreet, who after the war had a number of conflicts with Early, wrote that he considered Early "the weakest general officer of the Army of Northern Virginia …" E.Porter Alexander disagreed: "Early proved himself a remarkable corps commander. His greatest quality perhaps was the fearlessness with which he fought against all odds & discouragments."

Lee, who called Early "my bad old man," gave him command of II Corps and ordered him to drive the enemy out of the Valley of Virginia and threaten Washington, DC. In July 1864, as Early started off, one of Lee's staff officers, Lt.Col. Walter Taylor, a religious man, wrote home, "Don't tell anyone I say so, but I have feared our friend Early w[oul]d not accomplish much because he is such a Godless man. He is a man who utterly sets at defiance all moral laws & such a one Heaven will not favour."

In fact, Early's men reached the outskirts of Washington before overwhelming numbers forced their retreat to the Valley. There they were followed by troops led by Philip Sheridan who defeated the Confederates at Winchester and Fisher's Hill. Early turned and struck the Union troops on 19 October 1864 at Cedar Creek. Sheridan rallied his men there and drove the Confederates from the field, following his victory with attacks that destroyed Early's army at Waynesboro, Virginia, in March 1865.

Early never held command again, and traveled to Mexico in disguise after the Confederate surrender. Later he returned to Lynchburg and resumed his law career. A strong supporter of Lee, he was a founder and first president of the Southern Historical Society, spending much effort trying to prove that it was Longstreet who had lost Gettysburg. He died on 2 March 1894 in Lynchburg, where he is buried.

EVANS, Nathan George (1824–63)

Nathan George Evans (see Plate A3) was born in Marion, South Carolina, on 3 February 1824. After schooling at Randolph Macon College he went on to the US Military Academy, and was graduated 36th in the 38-strong class of 1848. It was while at West Point that Evans gained the nickname "Shanks," due to the thinness of his legs. Commissioned into the dragoons, Evans served on the western frontier from 1849 to 1861. He resigned from the army as a captain in February 1861 to follow his state's fortunes.

Made a colonel, Evans was in command of a brigade on the extreme left of the Confederate line at First Manassas (Bull Run) on 21 July 1861. There he discovered the Union flanking attack and rapidly redeployed to meet this threat; his actions were one of the most important factors in the Confederate victory. Sent to command in northern Virginia along the Potomac River, he was headquartered in Leesburg when Federal troops under Edward Baker attempted to cross the river at nearby Balls Bluff and attack his camp on 21 October. Evans reacted quickly and decisively to drive the invading force into the Potomac, for which action he received the thanks of the Confederate Congress and a gold medal from South Carolina. He was also promoted to brigadier-general with effect from the date of the engagement. One of the captured Federal officers from Balls Bluff, Lt. William Harris of the 71st Pennsylvania, described Evans at this time: "(He is known throughout his command by the euphonious sobriquet of 'Shanks.') His manners are courteous and dignified, being to a certain extent free from that peculiar mixture of supercilious pride and conceit which characterizes many of the officers in the Confederate army."

Evans went on to command a brigade, known as the "Tramp Brigade" since it showed up under so many commands, that fought at Second Manassas, South Mountain, Sharpsburg (Antietam), in the Vicksburg campaign in the west, and at Kinston, North Carolina. At the same time, however, Evans gained a reputation as an especially hard drinker – in an army that was filled with hard drinkers. "Genl Evans is one of the bravest men I ever saw, and no doubt a good officer when sober," Longstreet's staff officer Capt. Thomas Goree wrote home after Evans' fight at Balls Bluff; "but he is unfortunately nearly always under the influence of liquor."

Eventually ending up in North Carolina under command of P.G.T.Beauregard, Evans finally ran into trouble. Colonel Johnson Hagood, whose regiment was under Evans' command in the Secessionville campaign, claimed that Evans did not obey orders to attack: "He was not court-martialed," Hagood wrote, "for then, as ever afterwards, it was the bane of Confederate service not to hold its commanding officers to rigid account. Evans attempted indirectly to clear himself of the slur upon his reputation by court-martialing one of his colonels for drunkenness upon this occasion, alleging in the charges that this drunkenness had balked the attack." Evidence at this

Arnold Elzy, a West Pointer who was breveted for gallantry in the Mexican War, was the first colonel of the 1st Maryland Infantry. Named a brigadier-general for his service at First Manassas, he was badly wounded in the Seven Days' fighting and was never able to return to front-line command. On his return to duty he was promoted a major-general (December 1862) and given command of the Department of Richmond. Towards the end of the war he was transferred to the Army of Tennessee as chief of artillery, but did not accompany this army into Tennessee after the fall of Atlanta. Instead he surrendered in Georgia in May 1865, and returned to Maryland after the war.

Richard Ewell in a regulation general officer's coat; see Plate G1.

trial not only showed the colonel guilty, but Evans as well.

Eventually, Evans was tried for intoxication by a court martial but was acquitted. Beauregard, however, did not like Evans nor trust his judgment. When Evans called for reinforcements in North Carolina, Beauregard complained to the Secretary of War on 6 January 1863, "it is dangerous to weaken forces here too much, considering [the] difficulty of getting [them] back in case of sudden attack by the enemy. I think General Evans must overestimate [the] latter."

Finally Beauregard relieved Evans of his command and placed him under arrest – though later releasing him – and asked the president to send him to another theater. The Confederate Army Adjutant and Inspector General, Samuel Cooper, wrote to President Davis on 7 January 1864 that he thought Evans should be sent before an examining board to see if he were fit for duty. In fact, Evans' military career was essentially over.

After the war he became the principal of a high school at Midway, Alabama. He died there on 23 November 1868, and is buried in Cokesbury, South Carolina.

EWELL, Richard Stoddart (1817–72)

Richard Stoddart Ewell (see Plate G1) was born in Georgetown, DC, on 8 February 1817. Appointed to West Point from Virginia, he was graduated 13th in the class of 1840 and was assigned to the dragoons. He received a brevet in the Mexican War, and was wounded in action against Apaches in 1859. He resigned his commission as a US Army captain in May 1861; and on 17 June was commissioned a brigadier-general in the Provisional Army of the Confederate States of America. He fought with distinction at First Manassas (Bull Run) in July 1861, and consequently was promoted to major-general on 24 January 1862. He was sent to the aid of Jackson in the Shenandoah Valley, serving under him there and when Jackson sped to the relief of Richmond in the Seven Days' Battles (25 June–1 July 1862).

Campbell Brown, Ewell's stepson and an officer on his staff, later recalled an occasion after First Manassas when Ewell and he stopped at a nearby house looking for buttermilk. Ewell asked the owner for a pair of scissors; and Brown was surprised to see him "pick up her scissors and begin cutting his own hair, without a glass or any guide except his fingers. He had half finished when she came out, and laid down the scissors, drank his milk and rode off with the hair on one side of his head cut short, on the other not noticed, but luckily not much of it at any rate and only an inch or so of difference – which I got him to have rectified a few days later."

Ewell saw combat in the Second Manassas campaign, and on 28 August 1862 was badly wounded at the battle of Groveton: his kneecap was split in two and the leg bone shattered, and the leg was amputated shortly thereafter. Fitted with a wooden leg, Ewell returned to service and was named a lieutenant-general to command II Corps of the Army of Northern Virginia on 23 May 1863 after Jackson's death at Chancellorsville.

Ewell was greatly criticized for not carrying the Confederate attack forward in the waning hours of 1 July 1863 at Gettysburg, when the Federal troops might have been forced off Cemetery Hill. Usually bold in the attack, he halted and allowed the enemy to consolidate, eventually surrendering them the good ground from which they would win the battle. Ill health forced Ewell's retirement in 1864, after serving from Gettysburg to Spotsylvania, and he would not return to the Army of Northern Virginia again. When able, he was given command of the defenses of Richmond, evacuating that city with Lee's forces on 2 April 1865. He was captured with most of his command on 6 April at the battle of Sailor's Creek. After being released from a short term in the northern prisoner of war camp at Fort Warren, near Boston, he returned to take up farming near Spring Hill, Tennessee. He died there on 25 January 1872, and is buried in the Old City Cemetery in Nashville.

Moxley Sorrel recalled of Ewell: "A perfect horseman and lover of horses (racers), he never tired of talking of his horse 'Tangent,' in Texas, who appears to have never won a race and always to have lost his owner's money. But the latter's confidence never weakened and he always believed in 'Tangent.'" John Gordon, who felt that Ewell was "the oddest, most eccentric genius in the Confederate Army," said that he "was in truth as tender and sympathetic as a woman, but, even under slight provocation, he became externally as rough as a polar bear, and the needles with which he pricked sensibilities were more numerous and keener than porcupines' quills. His written orders were full, accurate, and lucid; but his verbal orders or directions, especially when under intense excitement, no man could comprehend ... [although] woe to the dull subordinate who failed to understand him!"

GORDON, John Brown (1832–1904)

John Brown Gordon (**see Plate H1**) was born in Upson County, Georgia, on 6 February 1832. He was educated at the University of Georgia, although he did not graduate. He pursued a number of ventures thereafter, practicing law in Atlanta and developing coal mines in the north-west corner of the state. He married Fanny Haralson, a native Georgian, in September 1854, and the couple had two children by 1861.

At the outbreak of the Civil War Gordon joined a Georgia volunteer company of mounted troops, the Wilkes Valley Guards, who elected him their first lieutenant. However, as infantry was more needed than cavalry when the war began, the company voted to convert to infantry. Gordon was quickly elected captain of the company, which renamed itself the "Raccoon Roughs" and was taken into service from Alabama as a company of the 6th Alabama, of which regiment Gordon became commander. As such he saw service at Seven Pines (Fair Oaks, 31 May–1 June 1862), in which, he recalled, "My field officers and adjutant were all dead. Every horse ridden into the fight, my own among them, was dead. Fully one half of my line officers and half my men were dead or wounded." At Sharpsburg (Antietam, 17 September 1862) Gordon was shot five times; the last bullet "struck me squarely in the face, and passed out, barely

missing the jugular vein. I fell forward and lay unconscious with my face in my cap; and it would seem that I might have been smothered by the blood running into my cap from this last wound but for the act of some Yankee, who, as if to save my life, had at a previous hour in the battle, shot a hole through the cap, which let the blood out."

Nursed back to health over a period of seven months, largely by his wife who stayed with him at the hospital, Gordon was named a brigadier-general on 1 November 1862. Gordon's Brigade was one of the first on the field at Gettysburg on 1 July 1863, where he met in the early evening with Ewell and Early. He pleaded with them to allow his men to continue their successful drive. As he later wrote, "I did not hesitate to say to both Ewell and Early that a line of heavy earthworks, with heavy guns and ranks of infantry behind them, would frown upon us at

John Gordon wore a gray coat with white trim on the collar, cuffs, and front edge, with his buttons arranged in pairs, as per regulations.

daylight … There was a disposition to yield to my suggestions, but other counsels finally prevailed." There would be no attack on Culp's and Cemetery Hill, and the Union line, consolidated that night, would hold on for two more days of bloody attacks.

Gordon's command, part of Longstreet's Corps, went on to fight at Chickamauga and Knoxville in September and November 1863 before returning to the Army of Northern Virginia. His record thereafter was excellent, during both the Wilderness campaign (May 1864) and in Early's drive on Washington that July. In this latter march it was Gordon's troops who turned the Union flank and drove them from the Monocacy River, opening the way to Washington. On 14 May 1864 he was promoted to major-general.

Gordon suggested and commanded Lee's last offensive, a drive on Fort Stedman outside Petersburg during the siege – this would be the last time the Army of Northern Virginia attacked the Army of the Potomac. A combination of faulty Southern intelligence and a quick Union reaction doomed the attack, which failed with heavy losses. Petersburg fell shortly

Gordon in another view with the same coat. He wears a US Army general officer's gold and red sword belt, and holds a black broad-brimmed hat with a gold hat cord. His weapon is a cavalry officer's saber. See Plate H1.

thereafter; and Gordon, serving as a corps commander although not promoted to lieutenant-general, ended up commanding roughly half of Lee's troops on the march to Appomattox. Once there, Gordon led the surrendering Army of Northern Virginia to the field where it stacked arms and folded its colors for the last time.

After the war Gordon and his family settled in Atlanta. He became active in politics, working to have occupation troops removed from the state and home rule returned to Georgia. He was elected to the United States Senate in 1873 and again in 1891, and became state governor in 1886. He was also active in organizing the United Confederate Veterans, becoming its first commander-in-chief in 1890. He served as such until his death on 9 January 1904 in Miami, Florida. He is buried in Oakland Cemetery, Atlanta; and his statue stands in the grounds of the Georgia capitol building.

GREGG, Maxcy (1814–62)

Maxcy Gregg (**see Plate C1**) was born in Charleston, South Carolina, on 1 August 1814. He attended South Carolina College without graduating, and then joined his father's law practice. He was admitted to the state bar in 1839. Interested in things military, he obtained a major's commission in the 12th US Infantry in the Mexican War (1846–48). Mustered out at the war's end, Gregg returned to the practice of law first in Charleston, and subsequently in Columbia, the state capital, where the outbreak of the Civil War found him. He was a member of the state Secession Convention and was appointed by that convention as colonel of the state's 1st South Carolina Volunteers, which was sworn in for six months' service.

Gregg was present with his regiment at the firing on Fort Sumter and then led it to northern Virginia. In July 1861 the six months were up and the regiment mustered out, but Gregg and his two other field officers remained in the field to recruit a new 1st South Carolina that would serve for the rest of the war. In December 1861 Gregg was commissioned a brigadier-general in the Provisional Army of the Confederate States and ordered to return to Charleston. There he was given command of a brigade of five regiments of state troops, which he brought back to Virginia in April 1862. His brigade was assigned to A.P.Hill's "Light Division," with which it saw action in the Peninsula campaign of April and May. The brigade's historian later reported that, "Gregg's brigade suffered in these battles to the extent of almost a thousand men, which was little less than half the force engaged in the campaign." Nevertheless, it went on to serve in the battles of Cedar Mountain (9 August), Second Manassas (Bull Run, 29–30 August) the capture of Harper's Ferry (15 September), and Sharpsburg (Antietam, 17 September). Gregg cotinued to build his reputation in these actions; Hill called him "the gallant Gregg" in his report on Second Manassas.

Later in September Gregg's Brigade was withdrawn to Martinsburg and then to Winchester, Virginia, where it was resupplied and the men had a chance to rest and clean up. The unit was called to rejoin the main force near Fredericksburg, Virginia, in December, when a new Union drive threatened Richmond once again. Gregg's Brigade was posted in some woods on the right of the line in reserve, with two other brigades at his front. The men rested with stacked arms, brewing coffee on small fires.

There was, however, a gap of some 600 yards between the two Confederate brigades in the front line. "Unfortunately, Gen. Gregg was not aware of the interval between Lane's and Archer's brigades," wrote J.F.J.Caldwall, an officer in the command. "The interval was directly in his front. We could not see the front line, of course." The enemy struck Lane's and Archer's brigades and swarmed through the gap into the midst of Gregg's men.

South Carolinians in the first unit to be hit sprang to their feet and grabbed their weapons. "But Gen. Gregg, who was rather deaf, not being able to see the true state of affairs, and anxious to prevent firing into the first line of our own troops, (who must, in reason, fall back over us before the enemy could reach us,) rode rapidly to the right and ordered the men to quit the stacks and refrain from firing. In fact, he rode in front of the line, and used every effort to stop them." As he was doing this, "Gen. Gregg was, of course, an object of note, riding, in full uniform, in front of the regiment. The enemy fired upon him, and he fell, mortally wounded through the spine."

Gregg was carried from the field to a nearby residence, but died a day later, on 15 December 1862. His body was returned to South Carolina, and he was buried in Columbia. At his funeral, "which took place in all due pomp, there was hardly a dry eye in that brigade," wrote staff officer Richard Corbin. "General Lee considered him the best brigadier in his army. Shortly before his death it was rumoured that he would assume the command of the lamented Rhodes's division, and a worthy successor he would have made to that able general."

HAMPTON, Wade (1818–1902)

Wade Hampton (see Plate C3) was born in Charleston, South Carolina, on 28 March 1818. A graduate of South Carolina College in 1836, he became the wealthiest planter in the state and was elected to both houses of the state legislature. When the war broke out he organized a legion consisting of an infantry battalion, an artillery battalion, and a cavalry battalion, paying for all the equipment – from cannon to uniforms – from his own pocket. He was wounded at First Manassas (Bull Run, 21 July 1861) at the head of Hampton's Legion. An old family friend, Mary Chestnut, recorded in her diary in March 1862 that among South Carolinians, "Wade Hampton is their hero. For one thing he is sober."

On 23 May 1862 he was commissioned a brigadier-general and given command of an infantry brigade, leading it in the Peninsula campaign. When Mary Chestnut congratulated him on his promotion he answered gloomily, "I was very foolish to give up my Legion." In July his branch of service was switched as he was given command of a brigade in Stuart's Cavalry Corps. He would serve thereafter in the cavalry until the end of the war. He was a friendly sort: his staff appreciated the fact that he brought along a game board for backgammon, drafts and chess for their use.

In February 1862 Hampton had caught the mumps seriously enough that consideration was given to replacing him in command, but he made a full recovery. On 2 June 1862 Maj. James Griffin, one of his field officers, wrote home that Hampton "was wounded in the foot painfully, but not seriously."

Hampton would again be wounded at Gettysburg in July 1863, and this time severely. Nevertheless, he recovered and was appointed a major-general, ranking from 3 August 1863, to command one of Stuart's two cavalry divisions.

Hampton displayed the typical prickly pride of the Southern upper classes. In March 1864 he complained to his friend Mary Chestnut that, "Stuart had taken one of Hampton's brigades and given it to Fitz Lee. General H complained of this to General Lee – who told him curtly, 'I would not care if you went back to South Carolina with your whole division…' Wade said his manner made this speech immensely mortifying …

"While General Hampton was talking to me, the president sent for him. It seems General Lee has no patience with any personal complaints or grievances. He is all for the cause and cannot bear officers to come to him with any such matters as Wade Hampton came."

Hampton considered his career in the Army of Northern Virginia finished and thought of asking for a transfer. However, Lee was above such matters of individual pride and, when Stuart was killed at Yellow Tavern, he gave command of the entire cavalry to Hampton. By this point resources such as replacement horses had become so scarce that a much better mounted and armed Union cavalry was able to outperform the Confederates in most of their encounters. Even so, Hampton served well, not

Wade Hampton – see Plate C3 – wore not only the regulation collar insignia but also the black shoulder straps edged in gold that were regulation for South Carolina's officers, although they had been forbidden in the Confederate Army. The former commander and "proprietor" of the all-arms Hampton Legion was the richest planter in South Carolina.

only keeping the Federal cavalry at bay but even managing one major offensive raid, the "Beefsteak Raid," in which his worn troopers captured a large Union cattle herd and brought it back to the main Confederate army, where it was much appreciated.

In January 1865, with Sherman's forces driving into South Carolina, Hampton was recalled to his native state to join J.E.Johnston in defending the Carolinas. He was given the rank of lieutenant-general on 15 February, to rank from the day before; Hampton was the only man to attain this rank in the Eastern theater who did not have a formal background of military training. On learning of this promotion Mary Chestnut noted in her diary, "Wade Hampton lieutenant general – too late. If he had been lieutenant general and given the command in South Carolina six months ago, I believe he would have saved us. Achilles was sulking in his tent – at such a time!" He would end the war in South Carolina.

After the war he turned to politics, being elected governor in 1876 and again in 1878. He was elected to the United States Senate in 1879, serving there until 1891. From 1893 to 1899 he served as commissioner of Pacific Railways. He returned to his native state thereafter, and died on 11 April 1902 in Columbia, where he is buried.

HETH, Henry (1825–99)

Henry Heth (**see Plate E1**) was born in Chesterfield County, Virginia, on 16 December 1825. Attending West Point, he roomed with Ambrose Burnside, and the two were constantly in trouble for disobeying Academy rules. He was graduated, last in his class, in 1847, and was commissioned an infantry lieutenant. Assigned to the 1st US Infantry Regiment, he saw Mexican War service. He was incorrectly reported killed while fighting Indians on the frontier in 1855, but actually survived. He was married on 7 April 1857; A.P.Hill was a groomsman. By 1861 he held a captain's commission, which he resigned on 25 April, to follow his state out of the Union.

Heth was named colonel of the 45th Virginia Infantry Regiment and saw service in the western Virginia campaign of 1861. Despite its failure Heth did well; he was said to have been the only officer in the Army of Northern Virginia whom Robert E.Lee addressed by his first name. Jefferson Davis thought a great deal of Heth, offering him a major-general's commission and command of the Trans-Mississippi army. Heth, although not noted for self-doubt, said that he first wanted experience at a lower level. He was promoted brigadier-general dating from 6 January 1862. He saw service in the Kentucky campaign under Gen. Kirby Smith, and was subsequently nominated to major-general's rank, but his nomination was rejected by the Confederate Senate. The problem does not seem to have been any disapproval of Heth personally, but rather a general feeling that there were too many Virginians among the Confederacy's general officer ranks.

Heth was finally assigned to the Army of Northern Virginia in February 1863 and given command of a brigade in Hill's "Light Division." At Chancellorsville in May, due to casualties, he found himself in temporary command of his division, performing well in the field. Heth was again nominated to the rank of major-general, to rank from 24 May 1863, and this rank was finally confirmed by the Senate.

Henry Heth, photographed wearing a plain gray officer's coat; see Plate E1.

Heth is best known for sending his division into Gettysburg town during the 1863 raid through Pennsylvania, and starting a battle there on 1 July. Heth told one of his brigade commanders to go into the town in search of supplies, especially much-needed shoes, apparently not knowing that Gordon's Brigade had passed through the town only four days before and picked the shops clean. Heth told his brigade commander that only home guard troops would be found there at most. In fact the Confederates ran into well-placed cavalry of the Army of the Potomac. Heth was incredulous at reports of strong Union forces present and, while discussing the matter, was joined by his corps commander A.P.Hill, who also thought that there could be no more than "possibly a small cavalry vidette." Heth, with Hill's approval, sent in more troops, although Lee had specifically ordered that a full battle not be brought on. He deployed his whole division, figuring that "blood now having been drawn, there seemed to be no calling off the battle."

Hill agreed, issuing orders for a further assault that afternoon. Lee, by this time having reached the field, spoke with Hill and Heth, telling Heth to "wait awhile and I will send you word when to go in" – an order that soon arrived. Federal infantry had come up, however, including the famous Midwestern "Iron Brigade," and the Confederates had a rough reception. Losses on both sides were heavy, but finally the Federals were forced back. As they retired through Gettysburg town a musket ball struck Heth in the head while he rode across the west arm of McPherson Ridge. Luckily the hat he was wearing was somewhat too big, and he had folded paper between the sweatband and crown; this cushioned the blow. Still, the general fell from his horse unconscious just as the fight reached its climax.

Heth recovered from his wound and returned to the army, serving until paroled at Appomattox. Moving to Richmond after the war, he took up the insurance business. He died in Washington, DC, on 27 September 1899, and is buried – like so many other Confederate soldiers – in Hollywood Cemetery, Richmond.

HILL, Ambrose Powell (1825–65)

A.P.Hill (**see Plate F1**) – whose ancestors had fled to America after serving on the losing Royalist side in the English Civil War of the 1640s – was born on 9 November 1825 in Culpeper, Virginia. His father was a businessman who was always interested in things military and desired young Ambrose to attend West Point. He was graduated 15th out of 38 in the class of 1847, having roomed with George B.McClellan while at the Academy. For a time he had been forced to drop out due to an unexplained illness, considered by some to have been a chronic liver inflammation, possibly hepatitis. He may also have contracted a venereal disease shortly after graduating from the Academy. Assigned to the 1st US Artillery Regiment, he saw service in Mexico and Florida. In Florida

An informal dresser, A.P.Hill wore a variety of uniforms including this civilian-style sack coat, edged probably in a yellowish buff and with the three stars of a colonel on the collar.

he came down with yellow fever, and thereafter he suffered bouts of this recurring disease throughout his life. Some, however, claim that Hill's periodic absences from duty were due more to psychosomatic than actual ailments. After a short time stationed in Texas, he was assigned to duty with the Office of the Superintendent of the US Coast Survey in Washington. There he courted the woman who eventually married his old roommate, Nellie Marcy; but a year later he married Katherine Morgan from Louisville, Kentucky. In March 1861, Hill resigned his commission to accept command as colonel of the 13th Virginia Infantry.

His regiment was in reserve at First Manassas (Bull Run), but he was still appointed brigadier-general on 26 February 1862. Fighting well in the Peninsula campaign, he was promoted major-general on 26 May 1862. He named his new command "The Light Division," although there was in fact no difference between it and any other division in the Army of Northern Virginia – the name was strictly a morale-builder. The division performed well at Cedar Mountain (9 August). In the 1862 invasion of Maryland, Stonewall Jackson, his corps commander, left him to take care of the surrendered garrison at Harper's Ferry while the rest of the corps joined Lee at Sharpsburg (Antietam, 17 September). Finishing that task, Hill double-marched his men the 17 miles to Sharpsburg, arriving

on the flank just as Ambrose Burnside finally got his Union IX Corps across Antietam Creek to threaten Lee's entire position. Despite large numbers left straggling, the 3,000 men Hill brought with him saved the Army of Northern Virginia.

At Fredricksburg that December, Hill's judgment in deploying his division was poor, leaving a gap in his lines that caused the death of Maxcy Gregg (see above). However, his over-all position was so strong that the Federals were unable to break it. When Jackson was mortally wounded at Chancellorsville in May 1863, Hill was given his command. He continued to direct the Confederate assault when he was

This is how most Southerners knew A.P.Hill: an illustration from the *Southern Illustrated News*, published in Richmond during the war. Cf Plate F1.

struck across the calves of his legs by a shot. Although there was no visible wound, his legs were severely bruised and even partially paralyzed: one of his staff officers thought a bursting shell was responsible. In a few minutes Hill was able to walk again and continued in command, but it subsequently became almost impossible for him to walk or ride, and he turned command over to J.E.B.Stuart.

On 24 May 1863, Hill was given command of the Army's III Corps and promoted to lieutenant-general. It was in this role that his troops ran into Federals at Gettysburg on 1 July 1863. There ill health struck him once more; he did not distinguish himself in this battle, and Lee even took some of his men to give to Longstreet for the attack of 3 July.

On 14 October 1863 at Bristoe Station, Hill struck a well-emplaced Federal force without adequate reconnaissance, losing some 12,000 to 14,000 men in the process. "I am convinced that I made the attack too hastily," he admitted later, "and at the same time that a delay of half an hour, and there would have been no enemy to attack." Lee never faulted over-aggressive behavior among his subordinates, and Hill retained his command. Although Hill's health continued to fail, he fought on through the Petersburg campaign.

On 2 April 1865, hearing reports of a Union breakthrough on his lines, he rode off with a sergeant to scout the situation. The two came across two Union infantrymen who fired on them, rather than surrender as Hill had ordered. One shot hit Hill's upraised left hand, taking off his thumb, and entered his chest, passing through the heart. The sergeant managed to save Hill's body; and he is buried in Hollywood Cemetery, Richmond.

Henry Kyd Douglas later wrote, "As a division commander he had few equals. He was quick, bold, skillful, and tenacious when the battle had begun; as at Mechanicsville he did his work dashingly and well. In the Second Corps he gained his chief glory and deserved the reputation he had. It cannot be said he added to it when he commanded a corps. Perhaps, like Ewell, who was probably his only superior as a division commander, after Jackson too much was expected of him." After the war Longstreet would write of Hill: "As a leader he was fine; as a wheelhorse, he was not always just to himself. He was fond of the picturesque."

Benjamin Huger was a West Point graduate who had served as chief of ordnance under Winfield Scott in Mexico. Quickly named a Confederate major-general on the outbreak of war, he evacuated Norfolk in May 1862, and did not live up to Lee's expectations as a divisional commander during the Seven Days' Battles. Relieved of his command in July 1862, he was assigned to duty as inspector of artillery and ordnance, mostly in the Trans-Mississippi Department – where Lee would occasionally send officers who proved unequal to his standards.

JACKSON, Thomas Jonathan (1824–63)

"Stonewall" Jackson was born in Clarksburg, now in West Virginia, on 21 January 1824. Poorly educated, he was still graduated 17th in the West Point class of 1846. Commissioned into the 1st US Artillery Regiment, he distinguished himself in the Mexican War, being breveted captain on 20 August 1847 "for gallant and meritorious conduct during the Battles of Contreras and Churubusco." He was named brevet major on

A portrait of "Stonewall" Jackson made in 1862 – his expression is less forbidding than in some other images. Kyd Douglas of his staff wrote: "He was quiet, not morose. He often smiled, rarely laughed. He never told a joke but rather liked to hear one, now and then." Note the plain gray coat with the collar stars attached on a black or dark bluebacking. Cf Plate D2.

13 September for his conduct at Chapultepec. Jackson resigned from the US Army on 29 February 1852 to take up a teaching position at the Virginia Military Institute. He also instructed African-American children at his local Presbyterian Church, of which he was a devout member. A Virginia militia colonel, he was named to command at Harper's Ferry at the outbreak of the Civil War.

Jackson was named brigadier-general on 17 June 1861, and took his 1st Brigade to First Manassas (Bull Run, 21 July), where his determined stand gained him – and his brigade – the nickname of "Stonewall" by which he has become known to history. Appointed major-general on 7 August, he was sent to West Virginia, but his poorly supplied troops failed to hold that part of the state. He was then sent to clear the strategic

Shenandoah Valley of Virginia of Union forces, and to divert troops from McClellan's army threatening Richmond. He demonstrated brilliant generalship in achieving this task; in his electrifying campaign of May–June 1862 his 18,000 men baffled, defeated, and tied down some 70,000 Federal troops by means of rapid marches and counter-marches. With the Valley now free, his forces were recalled to the defense of Richmond; but Jackson performed poorly in the Seven Days' Battles of June–July, and some believe that his lackluster performance was due to fatigue.

With Richmond safe for the time being, Jackson went north to stop a new Union Army of Virginia in its drive on the city, and his turning movement in August 1862 was the key to the victory of Second Manassas that followed on 29–30 August. In the subsequent Confederate invasion of Maryland he first captured Harper's Ferry, then sped to join Lee at Sharpsburg (Antietam), where his stubborn defense was central in saving the Army of Northern Virginia. Named lieutenant-general in command of II Corps on 10 October 1862, Jackson commanded the right wing at Fredericksburg on 13 December.

At Chancellorsville, Jackson suggested the flank movement that would smash the Union Army. On the night of 2 May 1863, while reconnoitering at Chancellorsville between two front-line North Carolina regiments, he was shot by jittery Confederate sentries. His left arm was amputated, but pneumonia developed and he died on 10 May. After lying in state in Richmond, he was buried in Lexington, Virginia.

Various images of Jackson made during his career. (Left) A Mexican War-period image of 1st Lt. Thomas J. Jackson of the 1st US Artillery (Library of Congress). (Right) An engraving of Jackson, made from a prewar photograph, that appeared in *Harper's Weekly*. The uniform was never a regulation Confederate type, but was superimposed on prewar photographs of a number of Confederate generals by northern photographers.

Charles Blackford, 2nd Virginia Cavalry, wrote home: "No one seems to know much of him, not even those who are with him hourly. He has no social graces but infinite earnestness. He belongs to the class from which Cromwell's regiment was made except he has no religious hypocrisy about him. He is a zealot and has stern ideas of duty." His men, noting this, called him at first "Tom Fool Jack," and later "Old Bluelight," as well as "Stonewall." Nevertheless, Kyd Douglas of his staff wrote: "He did not live apart from his personal staff, although they were nearly all young; he liked to have them about, especially at the table. He encouraged the liveliness of their conversations at meals, although he took little part in it As he never told his plans, he never discussed them." Jackson was concerned about his diet: Kyd Douglas recalled, "Whatever might be the variety before him the general selected one or two things only for his meal and ate of them abundantly. He seemed to know what agreed with him, and often puzzled others by his selections. I knew him to make a very hearty dinner of raspberries, milk and bread."

Later Blackford wrote: "He is ever monosyllabic and receives and delivers a message as if the bearer was a conduct pipe from one ear to another. There is a magnetism in Jackson, but it is not personal. All admire his genius and great deeds; no one could love the man for himself. He seems to be cut off from his fellow men and to commune with his own spirit only, or with spirits of which we know not." Perhaps this is why he was generally a poor judge of character, although he could certainly read an enemy's intentions.

The British military observer Arthur Fremantle wrote that Joseph E.Johnston had said of Jackson that he "did not possess any great qualifications as a strategist, and was perhaps unfit for the independent command of a large army, yet he was gifted with wonderful courage and determination, and a perfect faith in Providence that he was destined to destroy the enemy." E.Porter Alexander felt that this faith was actually a defect: "He believed, with absolute faith, in a personal God, watching all human events with a jealous eye to His own glory – ready to reward those people who made it their chief care, & to punish those who forgot about it."

KERSHAW, John Brevard (1822–94)

John Brevard Kershaw (see Plate G3) was born in Camden, South Carolina, on 5 January 1822. His grandfather had lost his fortune during the American Revolution and his father died when he was only seven years old. Having attended a local school and then the Cokesbury Conference School, Kershaw quit to become a clerk in a dry goods house in Charleston. Finding that boring, he became a law student under a local lawyer, and at 21 was admitted to the bar. He was married in 1844. In the Mexican War which began two years later Kershaw joined Company C – from Camden – of the South Carolina Volunteers, "The Palmetto Regiment," as a first lieutenant. However, once in Mexico he contracted a fever and returned home in poor health after resigning his commission on 19 August 1847. His wife nursed him back to health, and in 1852 he was elected to the South Carolina House of Representatives; he was also a member of the Succession Convention. Kershaw was elected colonel of his local militia regiment, which served on Morris Island, outside Charleston, during the bombardment of Fort Sumter.

It was then that P.G.T.Beauregard called Kershaw "a militia idiot." Later the regiment was accepted into Confederate service and sent to Virginia as the 2nd South Carolina Volunteers. On 13 February 1862 he was named brigadier-general in command of a South Carolina brigade.

Mary Chestnut had negative feelings about the general. In September 1863 she recalled how he offered to escort her though busy Richmond streets. People did not clear the way for them, however, "soon enough to please him. He called out, 'These must be citizens, not soldiers. They do not make way for ladies.'" On 4 June 1864 she ran into him again in Richmond, where "He was still pushing his own promotion, even to the point of being polite to me. As the Christians say, it was his own soul he wanted to save. I heard of nobody else's."

Famous as a brigade commander in "Pickett's Charge" at Gettysburg, James Kemper served as a volunteer officer in the Mexican War and then went into politics. Elected colonel of the 7th Virginia in 1862, he was promoted to brigadier-general on 3 June 1862. Badly wounded and captured at Gettysburg, he was unable to return to the field after his recuperation. He was made a major-general on 19 September 1864, and commanded Virginia's reserve forces until the end of the war. He was elected Virginia governor in 1874, retiring in 1877 and dying on 7 April 1895. This civilian-style costume is a good example of Confederate generals' sometimes individualistic choices of clothing and insignia display.

Fitzhugh Lee, a nephew of Robert E. Lee, was a West Pointer in the class of 1856; he became lieutenant-colonel of the 1st Virginia Cavalry in August 1861. "Fitz" Lee was appointed a brigadier-general of cavalry in July 1862 and a major-general in August 1863, receiving command of a division of Stuart's Cavalry Corps at that point. He assumed command of what was left of the cavalry after Wade Hampton was sent to the Carolinas in January 1865, and held it until Appomattox. He was commissioned a brigadier-general in the US Army during the Spanish-American War, retiring at that rank in 1901 and dying four years later.

Kershaw, a politician, understood his men well. Once when the brigade crossed the Rappahannock River in winter, the watching general called to his shivering men, "Go ahead, boys, and don't mind this; when I was in Mexico …" Before he could finish, one soldier called out, "But General, it wasn't so cold in Mexico, nor did they fight the war in winter, and a horse's legs are not so tender as a man's bare shins." Rather than punish the offender, Kershaw joined the men in laughter.

For continuing satisfactory service Kershaw was promoted to major-general with seniority from 18 May 1864. At Sailor's Creek on 6 April 1865 his division, then including some 6,000 men, was surrounded and most surrendered. Kershaw was sent to Fort Warren, from where he was released in July.

He returned to South Carolina and the law, being elected to the state senate in 1865. A member of the Union Reform Party convention, he prepared resolutions that recognized the Federal Reconstruction Acts for the state – an unpopular move with many ex-Confederates. Still, he was elected judge of South Carolina's fifth circuit court in 1877. Citing failing health, he resigned from the bench in 1893. He was then named US Postmaster in Camden, where he died on 13 April 1894. He is buried in the Quaker Burial Ground in that town.

LEE, Robert Edward (1807–70)

Robert E.Lee (see Plate D1) was born in Westmoreland County, Virginia, on 19 January 1807, the fifth child of Revolutionary War hero "Light Horse Harry" Lee. His father lost all his money and then died when Lee was 11 years old. While one brother went into the US Navy, Lee chose West Point, graduating second in the class of 1829 without a demerit on his record. Commissioned into the Engineers, Lee was sent to work on various seacoast forts until the Mexican War (1846–48). He also married, but his wife, Mary Ann Randolph Custis – who was related by marriage to George Washington – was later often ill and unable to follow him to different posts.

Lee served on the staff of Winfield Scott, the commanding general in the drive to Mexico City, and was slightly wounded at Chapultepec. He received brevets to major, lieutenant-colonel and colonel for "meritorious service" during the campaign. He was named Superintendent of West Point in 1852, serving until 1855 when he was appointed lieutenant-colonel of the 2nd US Cavalry. As commander of the forces at Harper's Ferry, Virginia, which suppressed John Brown's Raid in 1859, he was appointed colonel of the 1st US Cavalry on 16 March 1861. Lee would never take up that command; on 25 April 1861, he resigned his commission to accept the post of Virginia's chief general. He received a Confederate brigadier-general's commission on 14 May, and was then named a general to date from 14 June.

Lee's first assignment was to save the western counties in Virginia, but the badly supplied Confederate army, torn by dissention at the highest command levels, failed in this. Thereafter, he was sent to tour the south-eastern seaboard to examine defenses. Returning to Richmond in March 1862 to act at the president's military adviser, he was given command of the Army of Northern Virginia (which he named) on the wounding of Joseph E.Johnston on 31 May 1862. Thereafter he would remain with this force. On 23 January 1865 he was named General in Chief of the Armies of the Confederate States, but too late for him to affect the overall direction of the war very significantly. The details of his military career are available in too many biographies and analyses to be repeated in the space available here.

Richard Taylor, then one of Lee's brigade commanders, later wrote: "Of all the men I have seen, he was best entitled to the epithet of distinguished; and so marked was his appearance in this particular, that he would not have passed unnoticed through the streets of any capital. Reserved almost to coldness, his calm dignity repelled familiarity; not that he seemed without sympathies, but that he had so conquered his own weaknesses as to prevent the confession of others before him." Major Robert Stiles agreed: "He was of all men most attractive to us, yet by no means most approachable."

Robert E.Lee. After 1863 he switched to a plain gray coat with an open turned-down collar rather than the standing collar he had previously favored – cf Plate D1.

Lee, an elderly man during the war by mid-19th century standards, was often troubled by bad health. In early September 1862 he slipped while trying to catch his bolting horse, breaking bones in one hand and spraining the other so badly that he was unable to ride during the Sharpsburg (Antietam) campaign. He suffered a mild heart attack in early 1863, and was never wholly well again. Colonel Asbury Coward saw Lee in 1863 and again in early 1864: "I was struck by the change in General Lee's complexion. When I saw him the year before, his skin was a healthy pink. Now it was decidedly faded. He had aged a great deal more than a year in the past twelve months." By April 1864 Lee wrote to his son that he felt "a marked change in my strength since my attack last spring at Fredericksburg, and am less competent for my duty than ever." He was also tent-bound and ill for a time during vital fighting in the 1864 Petersburg campaign.

Various images of Lee
made during his career
and in retirement.
ABOVE
(Left) Lee photographed in
civilian clothes just before the
Civil War. This is how he first
appeared in Confederate
service, before growing a beard.
(Right) Lee was known to most
Southerners by this war-time
illustration from the Richmond
Southern Illustrated News.

RIGHT
(Left) Lee was photographed in
Richmond in 1863; this *Harper's
Weekly* woodcut made from the
photograph shows his usual field
garb, although it was noted that
he often left the sword behind.
(Right) A photograph of Lee
made in Richmond in 1863
differs from the woodcut in that
it shows a red-and-gold dress
sword belt and buff sash. Note
that the woodcut artist has also
given him a standing collar
instead of this open type.

TOP **After surrendering at Appomattox, Lee was photographed in his house in Richmond with his son G.W.Custis Lee (left) and his aide Walter Taylor.**
ABOVE **Lee was photographed after the war in his usual Confederate field uniform and mounted on his favorite horse, Traveller.**

ABOVE **Two images of Lee taken several years after the war when he was president of Washington College, Lexington, Virginia. The war had turned his hair entirely gray.**

In early 1864 Irishman Thomas Conolly met Lee, later describing his "large rich intense blue-ish grey eye, a beautifully shaped head, a most benign expression, manly healthful complexion, iron grey beard neatly trimmed, a nose slightly acquiline, a small well shaped mouth, erect with commanding porte & long graceful neck, solidly embedded in broad manly shoulders & deep chest the whole supported by a lightly knit muscular frame of more than the average height make together with an easy courteous manner one of the most prepossessing figures that ever bore the weight of command."

Staff member Lt.Col. Walter Taylor wrote home in March 1864 that, "My chief is first rate in his sphere – that of a commanding general. He has what few others possess, a head capable of planning a campaign and the ability to arrange for a battle, but he is not quick enough for such little affairs as the one I have described. He is too undecided, takes too long to form his conclusions. He must have good lieutenants, men to move quickly, men of nerve such as Jackson." The conventional judgement is that Lee was fatally short of such subordinates, and – ever the gentleman rather than the commander-in-chief – was fatally hesitant in controlling or replacing those to whom his delegation of responsibility proved unwise.

After Appomattox, Lee – who was regarded with adoration by most of his men, and complete respect by his opponents – retired briefly to Richmond. He finally accepted the post of president of Washington College (now Washington & Lee University) in Lexington, where he felt he could serve Virginia best by educating her sons. His poor health continued to plague him, however, and his heart finally gave out on 12 October 1870. He is buried on the university campus; and enjoys to this day a respect unique among the leading figures of the Civil War.

LONGSTREET, James (1821–1904)

James Longstreet (**see Plate A1**) was born in Edgefield District, South Carolina, on 8 January 1821. He graduated 54th out of 56 in the West Point class of 1842, and was commissioned into the 8th US Infantry, serving as regimental adjutant from June 1847 to July 1849. He was severely wounded while storming the convent at Chapultepec, Mexico, on 13 September 1847, and received brevets to captain and major for service at Contreras, Churubusco, and Molino del Rey. On 19 July 1858 he was commissioned a major and assigned to the Army's staff as pay-master. It was from this rank that he resigned on 1 June 1861 to accept a commission as brigadier-general in the Confederate Army on 17 June.

After fighting at First Manassas (Bull Run, 21 July 1861) he was promoted major-general on 7 October. His division was distinguished during the Peninsula campaign of April–May 1862, and Longstreet was named the service's senior lieutenant-general and I Corps commander from 9 October that year. In 1862 two of his children died of scarlet fever, and staff officer Moxley Sorrel recorded: "It was while we were about Centerville that a great change came over Longstreet. He was rather gay in disposition with his chums, fond of a glass, and very skillful at poker. He … [was] accustomed to play almost every night." After the children's deaths, for which Longstreet was present, he "resumed his command a changed man. He had become very serious and reserved and a consistent member of the Episcopal Church. His

1: Lieutenant-General James Longstreet
2: Brigadier-General Rev. William Pendleton
3: Brigadier-General Nathan Evans

A

B LEFT TO RIGHT   **1: Brigadier-General William Whiting**   **2: Brigadier-General Cadmus Wilcox**   **3: Major-General Gustavus Smith**

LEFT TO RIGHT   **1: Brigadier-General Maxcy Gregg**   **2: Major-General Lafayette McLaws**   **3: Major-General Wade Hampton**   **C**

1: Major-General Henry Heth
2: Major-General George Pickett
3: Brigadier-General Lewis Armistead

E

1: Lieutenant-General A.P.Hill
2: Major-General Robert Rodes
3: Brigadier-General
   E.Porter Alexander

2

1

3

F

1: Lieutenant-General Richard Ewell
2: Lieutenant-General Jubal Early
3: Major-General John Kershaw

G

1: Major-General John Gordon
2: Major-General Richard Anderson
3: Major-General William Mahone

H

grief was very deep and he had all our sympathies; later years lightened the memory of his sorrow and he became rather more like his old cheerful shelf, but with no dissipation of any kind."

After Fredericksburg (13 December 1862) his command was sent south of the James River, causing him to miss Chancellorsville the following May. Returning, his I Corps was active at Gettysburg on 2 and 3 July 1863, including the charge against the Union center – a move that he bitterly opposed, preferring to slip around the Union right. Afterwards Lee's apologists blamed Longstreet for attacking too slowly and hence losing the battle.

Longstreet's corps was sent west that fall, fighting at Chickamauga (19–20 September). After a disagreement with Braxton Bragg, commander of the Army of Tennessee, his corps was detached to besiege Knoxville. Failing to take that city, he had to retreat (4 December 1863) when Bragg's siege of Chattanooga was lifted. When Longstreet was sent to Knoxville, staff officer Charles Blackford wrote home: "Between us I am much afraid there is a want of energy in General Longstreet's management of a separate command. I would trust him to manage men on a battlefield as implicitly as any general in the Confederacy, but when not excited his mind works too slow and he is almost too kind-hearted to have control of a department … Longstreet is too phlegmatic to be efficient except when much aroused."

Returning to the Army of Northern Virginia, Longstreet fought well at the Wilderness on 6 May 1864; however, while he was riding along the front a Confederate regiment accidentally sent a volley his way, badly wounding him in the neck. His wounds, although serious, were not mortal, and he returned to the army at Petersburg. He was present at Appomattox for the final scene of the war.

Those who served with Longstreet often fell under his quiet spell. Captain Thomas Goree, a Texan on his staff, wrote in August 1861: "Genl Longstreet is one of the kindest, best hearted men I ever knew. Those not well acquainted with him, think him short and crabbed, and he does appear so except in three places: 1st, when in the presence of ladies, 2nd, at the table, and 3rd, on the field of battle. At any of those places he has a complacent smile on his continence [sic], and seems to be one of the happiest men in the world."

Those who had only a slight acquaintance found Longstreet off-putting. Francis Dawson, assigned to his staff late in the war, said that this duty was not "pleasant," since Longstreet "was disposed to be

In 1861 James Longstreet was photographed in the new regulation Confederate Army general's uniform, including here an unusually short tunic, with gold-striped dark blue trousers and a buff sash. See Plate A1. (Lee-Fendall House)

reserved himself …" J.E.B.Stuart's staff officer Lt.Col. W.W.Blackford wrote that Longstreet "impressed me then as a man of limited capacity who acquired reputation for wisdom by never saying anything – the old story of the owl. I do not remember ever hearing him say half a dozen words, beyond 'yes' or 'no,' in a consecutive sentence, although often in company with his old companions of the old army." One reason Longstreet gave this impression was simply that he was notably hard of hearing, and therefore did not like to mix in group conversations. Longstreet was known to his men as "Old Peter," the "Old Warhorse," and after Chickamauga "Bull of the Woods." Lee called him "My Old Warhorse."

After the war Longstreet moved to New Orleans and became a

A *Harper's Weekly* woodcut made from a wartime photograph of Longstreet in his mid-war uniform. This skillful engraving seems to capture the character of the subject with unusual sensitivity. In 1862 two of his children died of scarlet fever, in his presence, and the formerly convivial drinker and card-player returned to the army a much-changed man.

Republican Party member, which turned many ex-Confederates against him. A personal friend of U.S. Grant, he became US Minister to Turkey in 1880. He then served as commissioner of Pacific Railroads from 1897 to 1904. He died on 2 January 1904 in Gainesville, Georgia, and is buried there.

McLAWS, Lafayette (1821–97)

Lafayette McLaws (**see Plate C2**) was born in Augusta, Georgia, on 15 January 1821. He graduated 48th in the West Point class of 1842, six places above James Longstreet – with whom he would later have a difficult history. Commissioned into the 7th US Infantry, he saw undistinguished service in the Mexican War. He served as acting assistant adjutant-general of the Department of New Mexico from 1849 to 1851. Resigning his captain's commission on 23 March 1861, he was named colonel of the 10th Georgia Infantry.

McLaws received a brigadier-general's commission on 25 September 1861, and was promoted to major-general on 23 May 1862 for his showing in the Peninsula campaign. Thereafter he served well until the siege of Knoxville. On 17 December 1863, Longstreet, his corps commander, ordered him relieved from duty. On asking why, Longstreet's reply was "that throughout the campaign on which we are engaged, you have exhibited a want of confidence in the efforts and plans which the commanding general has thought proper to adopt and he is apprehensive that this feeling will extend more or less to the troops under your command."

In fact, Longstreet felt McLaws stood in the way of the promotion of Micah Jenkins to the command of J.B.Hood's division, a post left vacant when Hood was given command of the Army of Tennessee. In the event neither one of them was named to this command, but Longstreet continued to block McLaws' promotion – something that did not win him friends in Richmond. McLaws demanded and received a court of inquiry, in which he was charged with neglect and want of preparation at Knoxville. He was found not guilty of all but one specification, and Jefferson Davis disapproved the court's findings and ordered McLaws restored to duty. In the heated exchange of letters that followed Longstreet, backed by Lee, threatened to resign rather than have McLaws in his command. Rather than allow this to happen, McLaws was assigned a backwater post in Georgia. He thereafter served under Joseph Johnston, finally surrendering with him at Greensboro, North Carolina.

Major Robert Stiles wrote: "McLaws was rather a peculiar personality. He certainly could not be called an intellectual man, nor was he a brilliant and aggressive soldier; but he was regarded as one of the most dogged defensive fighters in the army ... His men were respectful, but not enthusiastic on this occasion [of a visit to their camp]. For the most part they kept right on with what they happened to be doing when the

After the war Longstreet put on weight. He became a Republican, and was a convinced believer in the necessity for the South to put wartime hatreds behind it and look to the future of the Union – a stance which made him unpopular with many other former Confederates.

General arrived – cooking, cleaning their arms and accoutrements, or whatever else it may be."

Another example of McLaws' easy discipline with volunteers came in Georgia, where some soldiers of the 1st Georgia Regiment (Regulars) were caught stealing a hog. In the words of 1st Sgt. W.H.Andrews, they were "carried to Gen McLaws' headquarters where the hog was taken from them, their names and regiments taken, and then turned loose threatening to deal with them afterwards. The boys lost the hog and never heard anything more about it."

After the war McLaws returned to Augusta, where he went into the insurance business. He was collector of internal revenue and postmaster at Savannah in 1875–76. He died in that city on 24 July 1897, and is buried there.

Thomas Munford, a Virginian, was one of those who rose to high field command in the Army of Northern Virginia without ever officially receiving such a commission. As colonel commanding the 2nd Virginia Cavalry, he was leading a brigade in Stuart's Cavalry Corps as early as May 1863, although he reverted to regimental command at several points before being officially appointed a brigade commander – although never commissioned as a brigadier-general – in November 1864. In early 1865 he was given command of a division in the Cavalry Corps, which he led until the end of the war. He brought his division out of the trap at Appomattox and disbanded it at Lynchburg after Lee's surrender. Although he never received a general's commission, he was photographed in this general officer's uniform.

MAHONE, William (1826–95)

William Mahone (**see Plate H3**) was born in Southampton County, Virginia, on 1 December 1826. His father, a tavern-keeper, sent him to the Virginia Military Institute, from which he graduated in 1847. He then became a teacher at the Rappahannock (Virginia) Military Academy while at the same time studying engineering. He subsequently left the teaching profession to take up railroading as an engineer for several Virginia railroads. When the Civil War broke out Mahone was the president and superintendent of the Norfolk & Petersburg Railroad. Although this would have been an important wartime post, he chose to enter the army, accepting election as colonel of the 6th Virginia Infantry.

Mahone was involved in the capture of the Norfolk Navy Yard before taking his troops to Richmond, where they helped to create the defenses at Drewry's Bluff. On 16 November 1861 he was made brigadier-general and given a brigade in the Army of Northern Virginia, with which he was to serve right through the war until Appomattox.

At Second Manassas (Bull Run, 29–30 August 1862) Mahone's brigade was in the part of the line hardest hit by Federal attacks; he himself was severely wounded, but his men held. His spirits seem to have drooped after Manassas, however. Lieutenant-Colonel Walter Taylor, who was close to a member of Mahone's staff, wrote home in August 1863 that Mahone "must be very unhappy & certainly makes those so around him …" After recuperating he returned to active service.

Mahone commanded a division in the Petersburg line when the Federals exploded a mine under the Confederates on 30 July 1864 and Ambrose Burnside launched an attack through the shattered defenses. Lee immediately ordered Mahone, whose division was nearby, to the defense of the line. Rather than send his men forward for another to command he dashed them up to the threatened line – which he knew from his railroad days – and sent them at the enemy with fixed bayonets. Leading from the front and under fire, Mahone displayed a personal bravery and close supervision of the counter-attacks that helped doom the Federal assault.

For his actions in this "Battle of the Crater" Mahone was offered a major-general's commission – for the second time. After an exchange of correspondence with Lee he accepted, and was appointed with seniority

The former railroad man William Mahone preferred short jackets with pleats in front and a fall collar, worn with dark blue trousers – see Plate H3. The meaning of the shield and star badge on his hat is unknown. Although a determined fighting general who distinguished himself at Petersburg, Mahone was particular about his diet, and his headquarters was recognizable by the milk cow and laying hens kept to provide food for his table. Confederate artillery battalion commander William Poague ran into Mahone during the retreat to Appomattox: "I found him sheltering himself under a poplar tree from a passing thunder shower and in a towering passion abusing and swearing at the Yankees, who he had just learned had that morning captured his headquarters wagon and his cow, saying it was a most serious loss, for he was not able, in the delicate condition of his health, to eat anything but tea and crackers and fresh milk."

from 30 July 1864. It was in the rank of major-general that he surrendered at Appomattox. Afterwards Lee said that of all the younger men in the army who survived to the end, it was Mahone who made the largest contribution to the army's organization and command.

After the war Mahone reorganized the Norfolk & Western Railroad while also entering politics. He lost several elections, but was finally elected to the US Senate in 1880 on what he called the "Readjuster Party" ticket. Essentially this was the local Republican Party, of which Mahone was the clear local leader. Mahone died in Washington, DC, on 8 October 1895, and is buried in Blanford Cemetery in Petersburg.

PENDLETON, William Nelson (1809–83)

William Nelson Pendleton (see Plate A2) was born in Richmond, Virginia, on 26 December 1809, the son of a lawyer active in both the politics of the American Revolution and the affairs of the Episcopal Church. The son picked a military career, entering the US Military Academy's class of 1830. There he became acquainted with fellow Virginia cadet Robert E.Lee, a member of the class ahead of him. He also came under the influence of the chaplain, who brought a number of cadets to the Episcopal Church. Three years after graduating from the Academy he resigned from the army and entered the seminary. Pendleton was ordained a priest in 1838, and was called to become rector of Grace Church, Lexington, Virginia, in 1853. Save for the four years of the Civil War, he would occupy this post until his death.

At the outbreak of the war he was elected captain of the Rockbridge Artillery, but did not stay long with the battery. He was soon made a colonel and chief of artillery of Joseph Johnston's Army of the Potomac, and was promoted to brigadier-general on 22 March 1862. Pendleton took every chance he got to officiate at Sunday services wherever he found himself, often begging civilian parishioners to support the army materially as well as spiritually. Indeed, he took care of himself materially as well; an artillery battalion commander recalled that during the siege of Petersburg, "General Pendleton on his inspecting tours nearly always dropped in at my quarters about dinner hour, knowing he stood a chance for a pretty good meal. No one enjoyed a good dinner more than he."

Pendleton was an old man in an army of young men and he was not as active as many desired. He took ill with malaria during the Peninsula campaign, and thereafter suffered from recurring bouts of the illness. For the last two years of the war his duties were largely confined to administration rather than field command. In this role he proved excellent in creating efficient organizations. He created the army's general artillery reserve, and took batteries away from infantry brigades to organize them into battalions. This turned out to be a distinct tactical advantage for the Confederates, who could mass their guns, although they were otherwise inferior to the Federals in the number and quality of their guns and ammunition.

On 15 June 1864, Lee wrote Jefferson Davis about the problem of filling the post of a corps commander with the Army of Tennessee: "As much as I esteem & admire Genl Pendleton, I would not select him to command a corps in this army. I do not mean to say by that he is not competent, but from what I have seen of him, I do not know that he is. I can spare him, if in your good judgment, you decide he is the best

William Pendleton, Lee's chief of artillery and an ordained Episcopalian minister, was occasionally confused for Lee by civilians when he was in Richmond – a mistake which gave the reverend gentleman much pleasure. Pendleton was liked but not very widely admired; E.Porter Alexander thought that "He was too old & had been too long out of army life to be thoroughly up to all the opportunities of his position." Nevertheless, his work in organizing the Confederate artillery for massed use on the battlefield was a genuinely valuable contribution. Cf Plate A2.

available." Davis, while he took Lee's advice and did not name Pendleton to the command, still thought well of the man. He wrote that in Pendleton "were happily combined the highest characteristics of the soldier, the patriot, and the Christian ..." At the same time Pendleton was scorned by his peers and subordinates. Sorrel dismissed him as "a well-meaning man, without qualities for the high post he claimed ..."

After the war he returned to Lexington, where he maintained close contact with Lee, who served on his church vestry. Pendleton died as the rector of Grace Church on 15 January 1883, and is buried in the church graveyard.

PICKETT, George Edward (1825–75)

George Edward Pickett (**see Plate E2**) was born in Richmond, Virginia, on 28 January 1825. He graduated 59th in a class of 59 from West Point in 1846, and was assigned to the 2nd US Infantry Regiment. He was transferred the following year to the 7th and then to the 8th Infantry, with which he served in the Mexican War. Not a brilliant soldier, he was nonetheless a brave one, earning a brevet to first lieutenant for meritorious conduct during the battles of Contreras and Churubusco, and to captain for gallant conduct at Chapultepec. He received a permanent first lieutenant's commission on 28 June 1849,

The dandyish George Pickett worn an unusual coat, although his trousers were regulation. This coat's non-regulation cuffs – see Plate E2 – as well as a sleeve from a coat that Pickett wore earlier, are preserved in the Civil War Museum in Harrisburg, Pennsylvania.

and a captain's commission in the 9th Infantry on 3 March 1855. Pickett was first noticed publicly as a company commander on the Canadian border during the "San Juan Island affair" in 1859. He avoided bloodshed in this border dispute and maintained good relations with his British counterparts while the affair was resolved.

Pickett resigned his commission on 25 June 1861 to join Virginia's forces as colonel in charge of defenses on the Lower Rappahannock. Appointed a brigadier-general on 14 January 1862, he led a brigade in the Peninsula campaign and was severely wounded at Gaines' Mill on 27 June. After recuperating he returned to the army in time for the Maryland invasion. He was named a major-general on 10 October 1862.

MAJ. GEN. GEORGE E. PICKETT.

A fairly crude engraving of George Pickett from the *Southern Illustrated News* published in Richmond during the war at least captured his long hair. The British observer Arthur Fremantle wrote of Pickett just before Gettysburg: "He wears his hair in long ringlets, and is altogether rather a desperate-looking fellow" – but then, Fremantle was judging by the standards of a Foot Guards officer of the mid-Victorian army.

It was Pickett's all-Virginia division, along with Pender's division, which were selected as being the freshest troops available for the attack against the Federal center on Cemetery Ridge at Gettysburg on 3 July 1863. The charge failed with enormous losses, and Pickett took it personally; when Lee, meeting him after the attack, told him to look after his division, he blurted out that he had no division.

Pickett was sent to command the Department of Virginia and North Carolina, including the lines around Petersburg. He returned to the Army of Northern Virginia when Union forces besieged Petersburg and his troops were amalgamated with Lee's. 1 April 1865 found Pickett enjoying a brief break from his duties, eating newly caught shad with fellow generals Thomas Rosser and Fitz Lee. His troops were on the far Confederate right, along Hatcher's Run, when the Federals hit. Although separated from his command by Union troops, he still managed to get back to his men at Five Forks; but his command was badly battered, and Lee was forced to retreat from Petersburg, going west and then south to join Confederate forces in North Carolina. Lee rather unfairly blamed Pickett for the disaster and relieved him of command. Pickett continued with the army, although without any official function, until Appomattox.

After the war Pickett went into the insurance business in Norfolk, Virginia, where he died on 30 July 1875. He is buried in Richmond. Longstreet wrote that Pickett "was of an open, frank, and genial temperament."

RODES, Robert Emmett (1829–64)

Robert Emmett Rodes (see Plate F2) was born in Lynchburg, Virginia, on 29 March 1829. He graduated from the Virginia Military Institute in 1848, remaining there as an assistant professor. In 1851 he resigned his post and became a railroad engineer in Alabama, where he was married in Tuscaloosa. He had applied for a post as professor of applied mathmatics at VMI just before the war broke out, when he returned to Alabama, being named colonel of the 5th Alabama Infantry.

Rodes served well at First Manassas (Bull Run, 21 July 1861), being commended for an action at Blackburn's Ford. On 21 October he was named brigadier-general in command of the brigade of Alabamans and Mississippians that had previously been commanded by Richard Ewell. Severely wounded at Seven Pines (Fair Oaks, 31 May–1 June 1862), he hurried back from his hospital bed in time to participate in the battle of Gaines' Mill. This return proved premature, and Rodes was forced to go on leave to recuperate on 27 June, leaving the field before the brigade marched off to the disaster at Malvern Hill. He returned to his post in time for the summer/fall campaign, serving well at South Mountain and Sharpsburg (Antietam, 17 September 1862). John B.Gordon, who served under him as a regimental commander, judged him a "superb brigade commander." At Sharpsburg, where Rodes' Brigade held part of the famous Sunken Road, his division commander, D.H.Hill, wrote that "Rodes' brigade has immortalized itself."

When D.H.Hill was sent to a North Carolina command, Rodes was given command of the division. He finally received the major-general's rank due to a divisional commander based largely on his service at Chancellorsville, where his division was in the van of Jackson's famous flank march. Rodes led his division at Gettysburg, after which he was praised by Lee – although in fact his division seems to have been badly deployed there. On 27 January 1864, Lee included Rodes on a short-list of four major-generals of whom he said he had "great confidence" in their abilities. Rodes led his men in the Wilderness and at Spotsylvania (May 1864); of the latter battle E.Porter Alexander wrote: "There were never, anywhere, two better fighters than Rodes & Ramseur or two more attractive men."

Brigadier-General Beverly Robertson, a West Pointer who served in the 2nd Dragoons in the West before the war, was elected colonel of the 4th Virginia Cavalry and then named a brigadier-general in June 1862. His cavalry command stayed with the main army instead of going with Stuart during the Gettysburg campaign, and Robertson's inept leadership was a major factor in Lee's moving into Pennsylvania blind to the enemy's dispositions. Afterwards Robertson was relieved and sent to South Carolina, where he stayed until the war ended. Here his coat appears to be basically regulation, with a general's larger center star on the collar, but lacks the Austrian knot in gold lace on the sleeves.

Rodes was sent with II Corps to the Shenandoah Valley of Virginia under Jubal Early in June 1864. He served there at the last battle Winchester, launching a counter-attack that helped trapped Confederate forces escape successfully. However, in the course of this action, shortly after noon on 19 September, Rodes, mounted on a fine black horse, was trying to control his mount while observing the advancing lines when a shell exploded nearby. A fragment struck him in the head, knocking him from the saddle. His staff and nearby troops rushed to his side but found that he was unconscious with a faint pulse that soon stopped. The land on which he died is now a housing development. Taken from the field, he was buried in Lynchburg.

SMITH, Gustavus Woodson (1821–96)

Gustavus Woodson Smith (**see Plate B3**) was born in Georgetown, Kentucky, on either 30 November or 1 December 1821. He was graduated eighth out of 56 cadets in the West Point class of 1842. Entering the Corps of Engineers, he was assigned to the Company of Sappers, Miners and Pontoniers in the Mexican War. He commanded the company from 10 March to 22 May 1847, and earned brevets as first lieutenant and captain for meritorious service at Cerro Gordo and Contreras. Afterwards he served as the Principal Assistant Professor of Engineering at West Point, and worked on various seacoast fortifications. Smith, known to army friends as "GW," resigned from the service on 18 December 1854 to become a civil engineer. In 1858 he was named streets commissioner of New York City, where he was prominent in Democratic Party affairs. On the outbreak of the Civil War he resigned immediately and went south to accept a commission as major-general in the Confederate Army on 19 September 1861.

Smith was considered a prize catch in the South, receiving universal praise as one of the top generals available despite the fact that he had never commanded anything larger than a company. He was sent to northern Virginia where he was given command of all troops not under Beauregard. Unfortunately he was not in good health. He quickly developed a plan to invade the North, but the Confederate government's strategy was one of strict defense and the plan was rejected. On 31 May 1862, Joseph Johnston, then commanding the army defending Richmond, was wounded and carried from the field. Smith, as the senior officer remaining, took command of the army. Initially the troops were cheered by Smith's appointment: "He is said, by those who know him, to be one of the very best men in our Army – and I am glad he has command," wrote Maj. James Griffin of the Hampton Legion on 26 March 1862. Longstreet's aide Thomas Goree took comfort in the fact that Smith was at least a "comparatively temperate" man.

After a brief talk with presidential advisor Robert E.Lee, Smith made a cautious return to Johnston's planned attack. However, on 2 June his adjutant had to report to Richmond that "General Smith finds himself utterly unable to endure the mental excitement incident to his actual presence with the army. Nothing but duty under fire could possibly keep him up, and there is danger of entire prostration. He goes to town today to gain a few days' respite. All business and all exciting questions must be kept from him for awhile. Major Melton will accompany him to prevent, while it is necessary, all such intrusion. Since writing the above I have again seen the general, and am pained to learn that partial paralysis has already commenced. The case is critical and the danger imminent."

An old acquaintance, E.Porter Alexander, noted, "I had always been a great friend of Gen. G.W. & believed him a great soldier. In the Mexican War he had been a lieut. in what was afterwards my old Co. A, engineers, & had an unusual amount of hard & close fighting, & he came out of the war with several brevets, & a reputation for personal gallantry second to none in the army. But some how, in our war, the fates were against him. He started with high rank but never had a chance in battle until this fight ... Smith was a martyr to physical ailments which greatly reduced his energy, &, especially made riding almost impossible. I don't know whether he intended to attack or not, but about noon Gen. Lee came out from Richmond to replace Gen. Johnston in the command."

In November 1862, Smith recovered enough to be appointed Secretary of War *ad interim.* However, when a number of generals who had been junior to him were promoted over his head, he resigned his commission in January 1863. Thereafter he accepted a commission of major-general of Georgia Militia, where he volunteered to design defensive lines, and organized that state's forces. He handled them well, especially on the Chattahoochee before the battle of Atlanta and later at the defense of Savannah in December 1864. He surrendered at Macon, Georgia, on 20 April 1865.

After the war Smith served as insurance commissioner of Kentucky from 1870 to 1876. He then moved to New York City, where he died on 24 June 1896. He is buried in New London, Connecticut.

STUART, James Ewell Brown (1833-64)

"Jeb" Stuart (**see Plate D3**) was born in Patrick County, Virginia, on 6 February 1833. He graduated 13th of 46 members of the West Point class of 1854, which was led by Robert E.Lee's son, George Washington Custis Lee. He was assigned to the Regiment of Mounted Riflemen, later serving in the 1st Cavalry Regiment, largely in Kansas. When Virginia left the Union he resigned his commission to become colonel of the 1st Virginia Cavalry. Leading his men into Union lines without direct orders at First Manassas (Bull Run, 21 July 1861), the young colonel rapidly caught the public eye and was promoted brigadier-general on 24 September. Virginia cavalry officer Charles Blackford wrote home after First Manassas: "Stuart sleeps every night on Munson's Hill without

Much was expected of Gustavus Woodson Smith, photographed here just before the war (cf Plate B3). He had been one of the intellectual stars of the prewar Corps of Engineers, and had proved his courage in the field during the Mexican War. However, in June 1862 he suffered a nervous breakdown as soon as he came under the pressure of senior field command.

even a blanket under or over him. He is very young, only twenty-eight but he seems a most capable soldier, never resting, always vigilant, always active." Stuart led the Army of Northern Virginia's cavalry on a reconnaissance right round the entire Army of the Potomac just before the Seven Days' Battles in late June 1862, a feat that gained him even more fame – and he played up to it. He was very conscious of appearances; staff officer W.W. Blackford noted that "General Stuart always dressed well and was well mounted, and he liked his staff to do the same. In our grey uniforms, cocked felt hats, long black plumes, top boots and polished accoutrements, mounted on superb horses, the General and his staff certainly presented a dashing appearance."

The visiting Austrian officer Fitzgerald Ross noted: "General Stuart is an absolute teetotaler, and never drinks anything stronger than lemonade. He says that if he were to drink any strong liquors at all, he is sure he should be too fond of it, and therefore prefers total abstinence. Nor does he ever smoke." Despite this, Ross added, "Stuart's camp is always one of the jolliest; as the General is very fond of music and singing, and is always gay and in good spirits himself, and when he laughs heartily, as frequently happens, he winds up with a shout very cheering to hear." For all that, Stuart was a devout Episcopalian.

The army's cavalry was enlarged to divisional strength and Stuart was named its commander with the rank of major-general on 25 July 1862. Later this command would grow to corps size with two divisions. Stuart, however, much to his chagrin, was never named a lieutenant-general to match the infantry corps commanders. He performed well at Second Manassas in August 1862, where his troops raided the enemy's communications and learned the strength and disposition of Union forces. He also distinguished himself during the Maryland invasion the following month, and his horse artillery was of great service at Fredericksburg in December 1862.

After Jackson's wounding at Chancellorsville, Stuart was given temporary command of II Corps, which he led well enough. However, shortly thereafter he gave way to vanity and staged a grand review of his corps for Lee and Richmond civilians, neglecting to post adequate guards. His troops were caught unprepared by a suddenly aggressive Union cavalry under Alfred Pleasanton at Brandy Station on 9 June 1863. Never again would Union cavalry be outclassed by Stuart's troopers. Stuart's pride was hurt, and he determined to regain his glory during the Gettysburg campaign.

Roaming around Maryland and Pennsylvania, capturing a large Union supply train that further slowed his progress, Stuart was out of touch with Lee's army during the vital days when it collided with the Army of the Potomac at Gettysburg. Lee had to fight without the information that only his cavalry could have provided, with serious consequences. With his usual indulgence, however, Lee did not relieve Stuart of his command. Stuart served well in the Wilderness in May 1864, managing to reach vital crossroads and protect Richmond from a strong cavalry thrust led by Philip Sheridan. On 11 May he was mortally wounded at Yellow Tavern during one of those fights. Taken to Richmond, where he refused a drink of whisky even though dying, he succumbed the next day, and was buried in the Confederate capital's Hollywood Cemetery.

Staff officer Kyd Douglas felt that Stuart was the greatest cavalry commander of the war, with the possible exception of Nathan Bedford Forrest in the Western theater: "Fond of show and with much personal vanity, craving admiration in the parlor as well as on the field, with a taste for music and poetry and song, desiring as much the admiration of handsome women as of intelligent men, with full appreciation of his own well-won eminence – these personal foibles, if they may be called such, did not detract from his personal popularity or his great usefulness."

Major Edward McDonald, 11th Virginia Cavalry, wrote of Stuart after the war: "He was the most brilliant cavalry officer of our army, greatly beloved by both officers and men, and a great loss to the army. His only

This *Harper's Weekly* woodcut of Stuart was copied from a photograph made at the same sitting as the photograph opposite, but has been "flipped" in the process of engraving – though a correction has been made to show the vest buttoning in the right direction. It is worth repeating that these woodcuts were not transferred from the original photograph or artwork by any mechanical process, but were manually engraved onto blocks of smooth-grained boxwood by the skill of hand and eye.

fault was in his love of dash and enterprise, often overtaxing the strength of his command in a fruitless raid. He ought to have more carefully husbanded the men and horses of his command."

WHITING, William Henry Chase (1824–65)

William Henry Chase Whiting (**see Plate B1**), one of the few Confederate generals whose performance never lived up to his promise, was born in Biloxi, Mississippi, on 22 March 1824. He not only graduated first in his class of 41 from West Point in 1845, but his academic record there was the highest ever achieved. Assigned to the Corps of Engineers, he spent the years from 1845 to 1850 overseeing the creation of harbor defenses in Florida and Texas, thereby missing the chance of action in the Mexican War (1846–48). In February 1861 he resigned from the US Army to accept a commission in the Regular Army of the Confederate States as major of engineers. He was appointed chief engineer of the Army of the Shenandoah, and did the necessary staff work to get that force united with the Army of the Potomac just in time for First Manassas (Bull Run, 21 July 1861). Jefferson Davis promoted him a brigadier-general on the spot, to rank from the date of that battle.

Despite never having commanded troops before, Whiting comported himself in an "Old Army" way which was most noticeable in a volunteer army. "Genl Whiting is pretty strict – brings us down to oats," Maj. James Griffin wrote home from one of his regiments in March 1862. "The men abuse him a great deal – but I think it is a good thing. Volunteers always abuse an Officer if he does his duty, and enforces discipline. But it amounts to nothing. Of one thing I am fully convinced, that an army undisciplined is very unreliable and almost worthless. Men must respect and fear their Officers, to be very effective." Staff officer Kyd Douglas noted that Whiting was "a quick-tempered, as well as an excellent officer …"

In September 1861, President Davis directed that the army's regiments be placed in brigades by state, where previously they had been brigaded for reasons of location, numbers, and so forth. Whiting protested when ordered to command a Mississippi brigade, calling this "a policy as suicidal as foolish." His regiments, he wrote, "are used to me, and I to them, and accustomed to act together." Whiting was consequently informed that his services as a general were not needed, and he should return to the post of major of engineers. Joseph Johnston interceded and managed to keep Whiting – who was going to resign – in the service. But Whiting had lost Davis' favor, and appears to have been doomed from that point on.

Whiting was blamed for not bringing off his equipment in a retreat from the Occoquan and the Potomac, and was asked for a detailed report on the subject. Even so, he was named temporary divisional commander when Gustavus Smith was moved up to army command and then left the army. Noted E.Porter Alexander, "Poor Whiting was a very hard drinker, & no one who knew him could but fear & wonder how he would acquit himself, off alone with his division ..."

Whiting commanded his division at Seven Pines (Fair Oaks), in the Valley campaign, and in the Seven Days' Battles. In this last series of actions in late June 1862 he was very critical of Jackson, while rumors spread that Whiting had been under the influence of alcohol and done less than his fair share at Malvern Hill (1 July). Whiting complained about these rumors, but Lee told him to "forget them, general; do not let us recollect unpleasant things; life is very short." Whiting went on sick leave in late 1862, and on his return found that Lee had arranged for his removal from the army and assignment to Wilmington, North Carolina, to defend the mouth of the Cape Fear River. As a sop he was promoted to major-general on 22 April 1863.

As his new department included defenses at Petersburg, Whiting served there for a short time in 1864. However, he failed to get his command into action at Port Walthall Junction, and again rumors of alcohol (and narcotic) abuse spread through the army. Returning to North Carolina, he was severely wounded and captured in the fall of Wilmington (22 February 1865). He was brought to Fort Columbus, on Governor's Island outside New York City, where he died of his wounds on 10 March. He is buried in Oakdale Cemetery, Wilmington, North Carolina.

WILCOX, Cadmus Marcellus (1824–90)

Cadmus Marcellus Wilcox **(see Plate B2)** was born in Wayne County, North Carolina, on 29 May 1824. His family moved to Tennessee and he attended the University of Nashville before being accepted for West Point, whence he graduated along with George Pickett and Thomas J.Jackson in the class of 1846, finishing 54th in a class of 59. He was commissioned into the 7th Infantry, serving as the regiment's adjutant to July 1847, before receiving an appointment as an aide-de-camp to Maj.Gen. John Quitman, whom he served until July 1848. He was breveted first lieutenant in 1847 for meritorious service in the battle of Chapultepec. Staying in the army, he was promoted first lieutenant in 1851, after serving in Florida in 1849–50. Although his academic record might not have suggested it, Wilcox became known as a scholar of war and was appointed assistant instructor of infantry tactics at West Point in 1852. He served in this position until 1857, when he returned to line duty with the 7th Infantry. Wilcox published several books during this time, including *Rifles and Rifle Practice* and a translation of the Austrian *Infantry Evolutions of the Line*. Wilcox resigned his commission on 1 June 1861, and became colonel of the 9th Alabama Infantry.

The 9th Alabama saw action at First Manassas (Bull Run, 21 July 1861) and Wilcox was promoted to brigadier-general on 21 October. Sick and absent during the Maryland campaign of 1862, Wilcox – known to his men as "Old Billy Fixin'" – commanded on the left of the Confederate line at Fredericksburg (13 December 1862) and consequently saw little action there. At the beginning of May 1863 he proved his value when he observed Union troops heading towards Chancellorsville in Lee's rear, and deployed his brigade successfully to delay the Federal advance while sending word back to Lee of this probe. His actions made it possible for Early to reconcentrate his scattered forces and protect the main army.

Wilcox's troops were sent to the right of the main assault on the third day of Gettysburg (3 July 1863), crossing the Emmitsburg Road but running into heavy Union opposition that checked them and forced their retreat. As Lee rode up to Wilcox's retiring forces, the British observer Col. Arthur Fremantle saw the two meet and Wilcox "explain, almost crying, the state of his brigade. General Lee immediately shook hands with him and said cheerfully, 'Never mind, General, all this has been MY fault – it is I that have lost this fight, and you must help me out of it in the best way you can."

Lee went on to recommend Wilcox to replace Dorsey Pender on the latter's death, writing that "General Wilcox is one of the oldest brigadiers in the service, a highly capable officer, has served from the commencement of the war and deserves promotion. Being an officer of the regular army he is properly assignable anywhere." On 13 August 1863, Wilcox was named a major-general, to the general approval of the army. His stubborn defensive fighting helped save the day at the Wilderness; and again at Fort Gregg in the Petersburg lines on 2 April 1865, where his stand allowed Longstreet to get into a new position to cover the army's lines of retreat.

After the war Wilcox moved to Washington, DC. In 1886 he was appointed land chief of the railroad division of the Land Office, holding that post until his death on 2 December 1890. He is buried in Oak Hill Cemetery in Washington.

Dr Thomas H. Williams was the first medical director of the army in Virginia, serving in that post until the battle of Seven Pines (Fair Oaks) in the Peninsula campaign at the beginning of June 1862. His uniform appears to be generally as regulation, with the black facings of the medical branch, though lacking the gold lace Austrian knot on the forearms.

THE PLATES: EAST

A1: Lieutenant-General James Longstreet
A2: Brigadier-General the Reverend William Pendleton
A3: Brigadier-General Nathan Evans

Moxley Sorrel, chief of staff to Longstreet **(A1)**, recalled their first meeting: "Brig.-Gen. James Longstreet was then a most striking figure, about forty years of age, a soldier every inch, and very handsome, tall and well proportioned, strong and active, a superb horseman and with an unsurpassed soldierly bearing, his features and expression fairly matched; eyes, glint steel blue, deep and piercing; a full brown beard, head well shaped and poised. The worst feature was the mouth, rather coarse; it was partly hidden, however, by his ample beard." Thomas Goree described him in these terms: "He is about five feet eleven inches in height, and weighs about 200 pounds, has light hair, about the color of mine, with blue eyes; has a florid complexion, and a very amiable, soft expression of countenance. He wears a large, heavy set of whiskers and moustache, which hides the lower part of his face.

When on foot, and in citizen's dress, he has rather a sluggish appearance, but he is exceedingly punctual and industrious. Whatever he has to do, he does well and quickly. When he dresses up in his uniform and mounts his horse, I think that he presents a better appearance than any other man in the Army." He is depicted here wearing regulation general officer's uniform with the short coat shown in a photograph, and high riding boots.

Captain Charles Blackford attended a church service where he "heard the Rev. General Pendleton **(A2)** preach a very good sermon. His avocations were curiously mixed in his apparel. The gown covered up his uniform entirely except for the wreath and stars of a general on his collar which peeped out to mildly protest against too much 'peace on earth' and the boots and spurs clanked around the chancel with but little sympathy with the doctrine of 'good will towards men.'" The British observer Arthur Fremantle noted in 1863 that Pendleton "continues to preach whenever he gets a chance. On these occasions he wears a surplice over his uniform." He suffered from a disorder, *cacoethes scribendi*, which produced some remarkable facial distortions.

The hard-drinking "Shanks" Evans **(A3)** was described by Lt. William Harris of the 71st Pennsylvania as "a man of tall, brawny frame and unusual length of limb ..." He had light blue eyes and reddish-brown hair, worn long although thinning on top. His frock coat is cut longer than Longstreet's and worn open at the throat; he wears no sash, and favours a slouch hat for field dress. Despite his reported lack of arrogance, Evans was noted as having a savage look to him unless he were smiling.

B1: Brigadier-General William Whiting
B2: Brigadier-General Cadmus Wilcox
B3: Major-General Gustavus Smith

William Whiting **(B1)** – like Evans, a drinker whose habit caused comment even in a hard-drinking army – was described as a handsome man who, being aware of his social position and professional standing as one of the elite of the pre-war US Army, was somewhat brusque in his dealings with others. He wears a plain all-gray frock coat with eight buttons, and unwreathed stars on the collar; his trousers and slouch hat are also gray.

The late-flowering scholar and dogged defensive fighter Cadmus Marcellus Wilcox **(B2)** was described by Arthur Fremantle in 1863 as wearing "a short round jacket and a battered straw hat"; the jacket has a line of white trim and three buttons on each cuff. He was of short stature, and photos show high cheekbones, a lined forehead and very dark eyes. He is shown here with a holstered pistol and cap pouch on his sword belt, and a black haversack and binocular case slung around his body.

A formal type of man, "G.W." Smith **(B3)** was photographed in regulation dress. He was tall, powerfully built, with massive, rough-hewn features that included thin lips, giving him a proud and even pompous expression; he was often noted as frowning.

A pair of binoculars made in France for sale to the armed forces in America during the Civil War. Binoculars were the most essential piece of field equipment carried by general officers. (Author's collection)

C1: Brigadier-General Maxcy Gregg
C2: Major-General Lafayette McLaws
C3: Major-General Wade Hampton

At the time of his death at Fredericksburg, Maxcy Gregg **(C1)** was 48 years old, of short stature, with blue eyes and dark brown beard and hair. He was described as wearing full uniform, and photographed in this gray "tricorn" – a hat associated with troops from Mississippi in 1861 more than those from South Carolina; the frontal decoration was a cockade of folded gold ribbons.

Of Longstreet's bête noire McLaws **(C2)**, Maj. Robert Stiles wrote: "His entire make-up, physical, mental and moral, was solid, even stoic. In figure he was short, stout, square-shouldered, deep-chested, strong-limbed; in complexion, dark and swarthy, with coal-black eyes and black, thick, close-curling hair and beard. Of his type, he was a handsome man, but the type of the Roman centurion…"

The prickly Southern aristocrat Wade Hampton **(C3)**, who succeeded "Jeb" Stuart at the head of the cavalry, was noted by staff officer John Esten Cooke as wearing a "plain gray coat, worn, dingy, and faded …" rather than the regulation uniform. He went on: "The face was browned by sun and wind, and half covered by the dark side-whiskers joining a long moustache of the same hue; the chin bold, prominent, and bare. The eyes were brown, inclining to black, and very mild and friendly … The frame of the soldier – straight, vigorous, and stalwart, but not too broad for grace – was encased in a plain gray sack coat of civilian cut, with the collar turned down; cavalry boots, large and serviceable, with brass spurs; a brown felt hat, without star or feather, the rest of the dress plain gray. Imagine this stalwart figure with a heavy sabre buckled around his waist …" Note that he wears the regulation three stars on his collar, but a single star on the gold-framed black South Carolina shoulder straps. The fuller beard is from a photograph – see page 19.

D1: General Robert E.Lee
D2: Lieutenant-General Thomas J.Jackson
D3: Major-General J.E.B.Stuart

One of a number of Lee's **(A1)** attested uniforms – see pages 30–31. Lee described himself thus in June 1861: "My coat is gray, of the regulation style and pattern, and my pants of dark blue, as is also prescribed, partly hid by my long boots. I have the same handsome hat with surmounts my gray head (the latter is not prescribed by regulations) and shields my ugly face, which is masked by a white beard as stiff and wiery as the teeth of a card." Charles Blackford wrote: "Lee does not hesitate to avail himself of some of the aids of martial pomp, though perfectly simple in his daily life, walk and conversation … Lee wears a well-fitted undress grey uniform with the handsomest trimmings, a handsome sword and cavalry boots, making him the grandest figure on any field." Moxley Sorrel described Lee: "Up to a short time before Seven Pines he had worn for beard only a well-kept moustache, soon turned from black to grizzled. When he took us in hand his full gray beard was growing, cropped close, and always well tended. An unusually handsome man … The General was always well dressed in gray sack-coat of Confederate cloth, matching trousers tucked into well-fitting riding boots – the simplest emblems of his rank appearing, and a good large black felt hat completed the attire of our commander. He

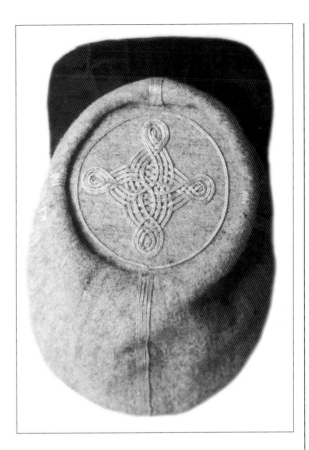

A reproduction of a Confederate general's kepi – in the gray which sometimes replaced the regulation dark blue – shows the elaborate "French knot" or quatrefoil of four bands of gold lace worked on top of the crown. The quarter-lacing at front, back and sides is also fourfold, while that surrounding the quatrefoil is single. (Courtesy William Wickham)

rarely wore his sword, but his binoculars were always at hand." In 1863 Fremantle wrote that Lee "generally wears a well-worn long gray jacket, a high black felt hat, and blue trousers tucked into his Wellington boots. I never saw him carry arms; and the only mark of his military rank are the three stars on his collar. He rides a handsome horse, which is extremely well groomed. He himself is very neat in his dress and person, and in the most arduous marches he always looks smart and neat." Private Luther Hopkins, 6th Virginia Cavalry, saw Lee in 1864: "He was dressed in a new Confederate uniform that fitted him perfectly, with long-legged boots, reaching above the knees. His collar was adorned on each side with three gold stars, surrounded by a gold wreath. His head was covered with a new soft black hat, encircled with a gold cord, from which dangled two gold acorns, one on each side. His full beard, closely clipped, was iron-gray, white predominating. I imagine that he was a little over six feet and would weigh 190 pounds. His eyes, I think, were brown, and as bright as stars." In the left background we illustrate Lee's headquarters flag.

Richard Taylor, one of "Stonewall" Jackson's brigade commanders, described him **(D2)** in 1862 in "a pair of

LEFT **A general and staff officer's sword made by Boyle & Gamble, Richmond. The star insignia is unexplained. (Author's collection)**

RIGHT **A drawing by a British artist of Jackson in an unusual overcoat, with his wreathed stars insignia on the deep fall collar – a non-regulation feature. The drawing was supposed to go to England, but was captured by the blockading Union Navy and used to make this woodcut for** *Harper's Weekly*.

BELOW **Drawing by a visiting British artist in 1862 of Jackson's tented field head-quarters and staff officers.**

were made of good material. His cap was very indifferent and pulled down over one eye, much stained by weather and without insignia. His coat was closely buttoned up to the chin and had upon the collar the stars and wreath of a general. His shoulders were stooped and one shoulder was lower than the other, and his coat showed signs of much exposure to the weather. He had a plain swordbelt without sash and a sword no respect different from that of other infantry officers that I could see. His face, in repose, is not handsome or agreeable, and he would be passed by anyone without a second look, though anyone could see determination and will in his face by the most casual glance – which I would say to fear but not to love." John Esten Cooke noted that "One of the most curious peculiarities of Jackson was the strange fashion he had of raising his right hand aloft and then letting it fall suddenly to his side." W.W.Blackford wrote: "Jackson was then about thirty-eight years of age, a little over medium height, of compact muscular build, with dark hair, and eyes that lit up on occasions with great expression, though he did not often indulge in conversation. Until after the battles around Richmond, his clothes looked as if they formed no part of his thoughts. After this period, however, there was a change; he dressed well and rode good horses."

Of "Jeb" Stuart **(D3)**, Col. John Mosby wrote that his "appearance – which included a reddish beard and a ruddy complexion – indicated a strong physique and great energy." John Esten Cooke described his costume: "His fighting jacket shone with dazzling buttons and was covered with gold braid; his hat was looped up with a golden star, and decorated with a black ostrich plume; his fine buff gauntlets reached to the elbow; around his waist was tied a splendid yellow silk sash, and his spurs were of pure gold." He added: "He wore a brown felt hat looped up with a star, and ornamented with an ebon feather; a double-breasted jacket always open and buttoned back; gray waistcoat and pantaloons; and boots to the knee, decorated with small spurs, which he wore even in dancing. To proceed with my catalogue of the soldier's accoutrements; on marches he threw over his shoulders his gray cavalry cape, and on the pummel of his saddle was strapped an oil-cloth overall, used as protection in rain, which, instead of annoying him, seemed to raise his spirits. In the midst of rain-storms, when everybody was riding along glum and cowering beneath the flood pouring down, he would trot on, head up, and singing gaily. His arms were, a light French sabre, balanced by a pistol in a black holster; his covering at night, a red blanket, strapped in an oil-cloth behind the saddle." In the right background we illustrate Stuart's headquarters flag.

E1: Major-General Henry Heth
E2: Major-General George Pickett
E3: Brigadier-General Lewis Armistead

The man who ordered the original "shoe raid" into Gettysburg town, Heth **(E1)** was described by the Irishman Thomas Conolly as "a most courteous, handsome man" who was "well appointed & rides a beautiful black stallion thoroughbred …" Of middle height, with light colouring and spare features, Heth wears two rows of nine buttons, set in threes, on his all-gray frock coat; note the frontal piping and open neck.

cavalry boots covering feet of gigantic size, a mangy cap with visor drawn low, a heavy, dark beard, and weary eyes – eyes I afterward saw filled with intense but never brilliant light … An ungraceful horseman, mounted on a sorry chestnut with shambling gait, his huge feet with out turned toes thrust into his stirrups, and such parts of his countenance as the low visor of his shocking cap failed to conceal wearing a wooden look, our new commander was not prepossessing." Charles Blackford wrote that "Jackson … was poorly dressed … though his clothes

A two-piece Southern-made belt plate as worn by generals and staff officers. (Author's collection)

RIGHT **An 1862 sketch of Lee by a visiting British correspondent formed the basis for this woodcut from *Harper's Weekly*.**

Of George Pickett **(E2)** – remembered by history, perhaps unfairly, only for the catastrophic final charge at Gettysburg – his wife recalled that when she first met him she noticed "his very small hands and feet. He had beautiful gray eyes that looked at me through sunny lights – eyes that smiled with his lips. His mustache was gallantly curled. His hair was exactly the color of mine, dark brown, and long and wavy, in the fashion of the time … His shirt-front of the finest white linen, was in soft puffs and ruffles, and the sleeves were edged with hem-stitched thread cambric ruffles. He would never, to the end of his life, wear the stiff linen collars and cuffs and stocks which came into fashion among men." Moxley Sorrel described Pickett as "A singular figure indeed! A medium-sized, well-built man, straight, erect, and in well-fitting uniform, an elegant riding-whip in hand, his appearance was distinguished and striking. But the head, the hair were extraordinary. Long ringlets flowed loosely over his shoulders, trimmed and highly perfumed; his beard likewise was curling and giving out the scents of Araby." Pickett was photographed wearing his coat buttons set in threes, and note the blue collar and gold-trimmed cuffs.

Lewis Armistead **(E3)** is depicted as he was described leading his brigade up Cemetery Ridge at Gettysburg on 3 July 1863, with his hat brandished on his sword. The only known photograph dates from before the war, and shows a thin man, conspicuously balding. Note the rank stars embroidered on a buff cloth oval sewn to the collar of the plain gray coat.

F1: Lieutenant-General A.P.Hill
F2: Major-General Robert Rodes
F3: Brigadier-General E.Porter Alexander
Chaplain J.William Jones described Ambrose Hill **(F1)** in 1862: "He was dressed in a fatigue jacket of gray flannel, his felt hat slouched over his noble brow …" Maxcy Sorrel described Hill as "of medium height, a light, good figure, and most pleasing soldierly appearance." In his first year at West Point Hill wrote that he was 5ft 9ins barefoot and weighed about 150 pounds. Hill was noted for wearing a bright red shirt in action, along with a regulation, gold-laced kepi.

Robert Rodes **(F2)** was photographed in a regulation uniform with white collar and cuffs. This gifted formation commander, praised by both his superiors and his subordinates, was six feet tall, thin-faced with a prominent, dimpled chin, tawny hair, and a long, drooping mustache.

E.P. Alexander **(F3)**, to whom we owe many comments on his brother officers, was generally photographed in informal uniforms with three metal stars pinned to his collar, rather than the embroidered stars which were the norm. Here Lee's gifted artillery commander wears a plain gray "sack" jacket with a turned-down collar, a broad-striped shirt with a bow tie, and trousers with a red seam welt.

G1: Lieutenant-General Richard Ewell
G2: Lieutenant-General Jubal Early
G3: Major-General John Kershaw
Campbell Brown, Ewell's stepson and an officer on his staff, later described first meeting him **(G1)** in 1861: "a medium-sized and plain man, with well-shaped spare figure and face much emaciated by recent sickness but indicative of much character and genius." Moxley Sorrel described Ewell as "Bald as an eagle, he looked like one; had a piercing eye and a lisping speech." Fitted with a wooden leg after being badly wounded at Second Manassas, Ewell was photographed as a major-general wearing this regulation frock coat with the buttons arranged in threes.

Of the stubborn and savage-tongued Jubal Early **(G2)** Moxley Sorrel wrote: "His appearance was quite striking, having a dark, handsome face, regular features, and deep piercing eyes. He was the victim of rheumatism, and although not old was bent almost double, like an aged man." John Esten Cooke described him as "a person of middle age; was nearly six feet in height, and, in spite of severe attacks of rheumatism, could undergo great fatigue. His hair was dark and thin, his eyes bright, his smile ready and expressive, though somewhat sarcastic. His dress was plain gray, with few decorations. Long exposure had made his old coat quite dingy. A wide-brimmed hat overshadowed his sparkling eyes and forehead, browned by sun and wind. In those sparkling eyes could be read the resolute character of the man, as in his smile was seen evidence of that dry, trenchant, often mordant humour, for which he was famous." He is depicted from a photograph, wearing his old "sack" jacket over a high-necked waistcoat and with the brim of his gray slouch hat turned up at the right. His headquarters flag is illustrated in the background.

Although the ambitious politician Kershaw (G3) was far from universally respected or popular, Moxley Sorrel described him as "of most attractive appearance, soldierly and handsome, of medium size, well set up, light hair and mustache, with clean-cut, high-bred features." Note the cuff detail, with a line of white piping instead of full cuff facing.

H1: Major-General John Gordon
H2: Major-General Richard Anderson
H3: Major-General William Mahone
Lieutenant-Colonel W.W.Blackford wrote of this much-wounded and energetic commander, responsible for the Army of Northern Virginia's very last offensive operation, that "Gordon (H1) was a very handsome man, well dressed, well mounted and with that indescribable air of a gentleman which is unmistakable." Note the cuff piping detail on the plain sleeve of his coat, and the cavalry saber slung from a red and gold dress belt.

Of Longstreet's quiet, steady deputy (H2), Moxley Sorrel noted that Anderson's "own meditative disposition was constantly smoothed by whiffs from a noble, cherished meerschaum pipe in the process of rich coloring. He was a short, thick, stocky figure, with good features and agreeable expression."

Sorrel described the fiery little hero of the Battle of the Crater in these words: "Maj.-Gen. William Mahone (H3) was a Virginian, about forty years of age. His appearance arrested attention. Very small both in height and frame, he seemed a mere atom with little flesh. His wife said 'none.' When he was shot (slightly) she was told it was only a flesh wound. 'Now I know it is serious,' said the good lady, 'for William has no flesh whatever.' Shallow of feature, sharp of eye, and very active in movement was the general; in dress quite unconventional, he affected jackets rather than coats, and on a certain hot summer's day that I recall he was seen, a major-general indeed, but wonderfully accoutrered! A plaited brown linen jacket, buttoned to trousers, of same material, like a boy's; topped off by a large Panama straw hat of the finest and most beautiful texture, met our eyes, and I must say he looked decidedly comfortable. But not always was he thus attired. He could be strictly uniformed when he chose." This pleated gray jacket is from the well-known photograph on page 47.

Robert E. Lee lived in this plantation house across the
Potomac River from Washington, DC. Captured early in the
war, the estate was used as a graveyard for Union soldiers,
and forms the basis of today's Arlington National Cemetery.

PART 2
CONFEDERATE LEADERS IN THE WEST

A woodcut made from the series of photos taken of Pierre Beauregard wearing Louisiana uniform in 1861. This appeared in the 27 April 1861 issue of *Harper's Weekly*.

INTRODUCTION

THE CONFEDERACY LOST ITS WAR in the West, and in no other theater did the conduct of individual commanding generals make so much difference to the outcome of operations. Firstly, the Union Army fielded its best generals in the West early in the war, and such figures as Ulysses S.Grant, William T.Sherman, and Philip Sheridan made their names there. Secondly, the group of Confederate generals who opposed them were of very varied talents. While there were some excellent general officers among them, too many attained levels of high command for which they were ill suited; the Condederate President Jefferson Davis remained a loyal friend, appointing them to their posts and retaining them long after he should have given way to public opposition. In many cases the generals concerned also regarded their own abilities more highly than they warranted.

Thirdly, many of the senior Confederate generals in the West quarreled with one another, and their consequent failure to co-operate often had damaging results. Jefferson Davis disliked Pierre Beauregard, Sterling Price, and Joseph Johnston, and the feeling was mutual. John Bell Hood plotted to replace Joseph Johnston, while William Hardee had no use for Hood and made every effort to get out from under his command. Leonidas Polk, Hardee, Daniel Hill and others plotted to replace their commander, Braxton Bragg, and at a fiery meeting Nathan Bedford Forrest flatly told that unappealing character that he would not obey his orders. Richard Taylor disliked Kirby Smith, and schemed to avoid having to continue serving under him. There was no "Western Robert E.Lee" whose qualities towered over those of his subordinates, giving him the authority to override their egos and keep them to their collective duty.

At the same time many generals of real quality, such as Forrest, Patrick Cleburne and Alexander Stewart, who lacked presidential connections and West Point education, were never appointed to posts of responsibility for which they were well qualified. Hardee, one of the most knowledgeable soldiers in the pre-war US Army, declined appointment to high command, although more qualified than many who accepted such posts.

The influence of the Eastern theater on Western generals was significant. At first Davis appointed Albert Sidney Johnston to oversee everything in the Western theater and, feeling that he had entrusted the task to the best man in the country, began to ignore the West and to concentrate on Eastern operations. After Johnston's death, Davis, a Mississippi native and deeply interested in affairs there, became very involved in the command structure and problems in that part of the

Confederacy. He actually traveled west to meet with his generals and tried to impose sort of order on the divisive squabbling that he found there. As a West Point graduate himself, however, Davis was greatly in favor of fellow cadets for high command positions, and often tended to advance them over non-professional soldiers of superior talents.

At the same time Robert E. Lee, as well as Davis, used the West as a dumping ground for generals whom they distrusted. Lee got rid of Magruder in that way, while Davis moved Beauregard to the West after that general's public criticism of the president following First Manassas. While these were good enough generals, they tended to block the promotion of local leaders who could have achieved more in that theater.

Portrait photograph of the handsome and elegant P.G.T. Beauregard in the uniform of an officer in the Louisiana State Army, taken in 1861. Note the style of fastening only the top button of the coat; if the image-conscious Beauregard chose to pose this way, we may be sure it was the height of fashion. *(Military Images Magazine)*

BIOGRAPHIES: WEST

BEAUREGARD, Pierre Gustav Touton (1818–93)

P.G. Touton-Beauregard **(see Plate A2)** was born on 28 May 1818, the son of a southern Louisiana sugar planter, in St Bernard Parish. At the age of 12 he was sent to boarding school in New York, where he first learned English. The school was run by two French veterans of Napoleon's army; the boy became fascinated with the military and determined, against family wishes and despite a chronic throat ailment, to attend West Point. There he took Beauregard as his family name, keeping the first part as a separate middle name. A good student, he was graduated second out of 45 members of the class of 1838 and assigned to the Corps of Engineers.

In 1841 he married the daughter of another Louisiana planter. When the Mexican War broke out he was named to Winfield Scott's staff, and was with the first troops to enter Mexico City. Thereafter he went on sick leave; when he returned he was assigned to Louisiana defenses on the Mississippi River. Beauregard's wife died in childbirth in 1850; but he soon remarried another French Creole lady, the sister of an important politician, John Slidell.

In January 1861, Beauregard was named superintendent of West Point, where he told a Louisiana cadet during the secession crisis: "Watch me; when I jump, you jump. What's the use of jumping too soon?" He was relieved from his post only a few days after being appointed, but he did not actually jump from the US Army to the Louisiana Army until 20 February 1861. Annoyed to be offered only a colonel's commission, he joined a socially prominent militia company, the Orleans Guards, as a private. His brother-in-law spoke for him, however; on 26 February he met with Confederate President Jefferson Davis, and on 1 March he was commissioned the Confederacy's first brigadier-general, with command in Charleston, South Carolina. He gained national fame by his firing on Fort Sumter, and later by his command at First Manassas (Bull Run) in July. He was appointed a full general to rank from 21 July 1861.

Beauregard, however, was his own worst enemy. Quick to resent any perceived offense to his honor, and already disliking Jefferson Davis (who had been against his taking the West Point command), his claim that he could have taken Washington after First Manassas, but was prevented from doing so by Davis, reached the newspapers. Moreover, he continually criticized Davis' friend and appointee Commissary General Lucius Northrup. Davis sharply rebuked Beauregard, and Beauregard replied not to Davis but via a Richmond newspaper editor.

Davis decided that Beauregard would be of more help in the Western theater; and the

Beauregard – center, pointing to his left – takes command after Albert Sidney Johnston was mortally wounded at Shiloh, 6 April 1862. *(Battles and Leaders of the Civil War)*

general arrived at Bowling Green, Kentucky, on 4 February 1862. As second in command at Shiloh (6–7 April 1862), he took over command of the Army of Tennessee when A.S.Johnston was mortally wounded and led the retreat back to Corinth, which he later abandoned as a stronger Union force approached it. Beauregard then left the army and went home without informing the War Department, claiming that he was ill. Davis took advantage of this extraordinary lapse to replace him in command with Braxton Bragg. When Beauregard recovered he was assigned command of coastal defenses in Georgia and South Carolina, where he did well, practising innovative approaches for defeating a superior enemy.

Recalled to command the defenses of Petersburg, he foresaw Grant's advance there before Lee did, and performed well in defending the city in mid-June 1864 until Lee could bring the Army of Northern Virginia around it. At Petersburg he greatly impressed his subordinate, the engineer and artilleryman E.P. Alexander, who later wrote: "Gen.Beauregard had more about him of what I would call military technique than any of our Confederate generals. He was very particular in the observance of all military routines, traditions, & methods, in keeping up scouting & secret service & in requiring reports & preserving office records. His records of the siege of Charleston, preserved by his special care & published by his surviving chief engineer, Maj.Johnson, would do credit to the staff of any European nation, and form the most admirable & valuable military narrative which the war produced. And the defense of Petersburg which Beauregard was now to make, is a real model of beautiful, exact & ship-shape play on the part of the commander, worthily backed by skillful administration in every department & by superb fighting by his troops."

Thereafter Beauregard was sent south, serving under Joseph E.Johnston until his surrender. After the war he served as president of a couple of railroads as well as supervising the Louisiana Lottery, and serving as the state's adjutant general. He died in New Orleans on 20 February 1893, and is buried in that city's Metairie Cemetery.

BRAGG, Braxton (1817–76)

Braxton Bragg (see Plate D1) was born in Warrenton, North Carolina, on 22 March 1817, to a father who was considered working class although he eventually owned 20 slaves. Bragg's ambitious father got him sent to West Point, from where he was graduated fifth in the 50-strong class of 1837.

Bragg was assigned to the artillery and saw service in the Seminole and Mexican Wars, acquiring a reputation as sharp-tempered and disagreeable with his fellow officers and something of a martinet with his men. As a light artillery battery commander at the battle of Buena Vista (22–23 February 1847), he gained fame when commanding general Zachery Taylor ordered him to "Double-shot your guns and give them hell!" – a quotation which reached the general public as, "A little more grape, Captain Bragg." Despite their service together in this battle Bragg and Jefferson Davis did not get along, and Bragg fought every attempt Davis made when Secretary of War to improve the army's artillery. Bragg, then a lieutenant-colonel, finally went to Washington in December 1855 to convince Davis of his errors; when he verbally offered his resignation in the course of this exchange, Davis quickly accepted it, earning Bragg's lasting hatred.

When Louisiana seceded Bragg was appointed the state's general-in-chief (much to Beauregard's disgust). On 7 March 1861 he was named a Confederate brigadier-general and sent to command at Pensacola. On 12 September he was promoted to major-general, with command of all of Alabama and West Florida. Concerned about the Federals in Kentucky and Tennessee, Davis sent Bragg and his troops north; they left Mobile on 27 February, arriving at Jackson, Tennessee, five days later. Bragg's command, designated second Corps, fought at Shiloh in April 1862. Even at this early date there was much dissatisfaction with Bragg among his troops. Private William Watson, 3rd Louisiana Infantry, recalled hearing a conversation among his peers in May 1862 in which "they were discussing the state of affairs and the action of General Bragg, and I heard something like propositions that the whole army should break up in a general row and march off in bands, taking their arms with them... ."

In June 1862 Bragg was given command of the Army of Tennessee and led it into Kentucky, a move that he botched by wasting time installing a pro-Southern government instead of moving against the Federal forces. These were led by the equally lackadaisical Don Carlos Buell, who beat Bragg at Perryville (8 October 1862) but failed to exploit his success. It was Bragg who failed to reinforce early success against Rosecrans' Army of the Cumberland at Murfreesboro (Stones River, 31 December 1862–3 January 1863), and thereafter he was forced

Braxton Bragg: an opportunity to compare the accuracy of an engraving made from a good portrait photograph. In 1863 a British visitor wrote of him: "This officer is in appearance the least preposessing of the Confederate generals. He is very thin. He stoops, and has a sickly, cadaverous, haggard appearance, rather plain features, bushy black eyebrows which unite in a tuft on the top of his nose, and a stubby iron-gray beard; but his eyes are bright and piercing." Note the curved cut of the front coat panel, and see Plate D. (Military Images Magazine; Battles & Leaders of the Civil War)

to leave Kentucky. Maneuvered out of Chattanooga on 7 September 1863, Bragg won a costly victory over Rosecrans at Chickamauga on 19–20 September, but once again failed to follow up, allowing the Federals to hang on to Chattanooga; Bragg besieged the town, holding strong positions on high ground. Grant arrived to relieve the garrison on 27 October, and on 24–25 November he drove Bragg off Lookout Mountain and Missionary Ridge.

At the latter engagement, Bragg rode among his routed troops trying to rally them. Captain Samuel Foster, of Granbury's Texas Brigade, noted in his diary: "He got down off his horse, and as the men ran past him, he called out to them not to disgrace themselves, but stop and [save] their country – fight for their families &c and says I (your General) am here. Just then one large man came past him who had thrown his gun away and stepped up behind Genl Bragg and carr[ied] him around the waist and says, 'And heres your mule', and went on." His men had had enough of Bragg. Robert Patrick, a clerk in the 4th Louisiana, noted in his diary on 20 January 1863: "Bragg is not fit for a general and I have always contended that, and the most he is fit for is the command of a brigade and he would make a damned poor brigadier. ... If Jeff Davis will just let Bragg alone, I think he will do us more damage than the enemy, and I believe that he is cowardly too. I know one thing, that he is a perfect tyrant, and I never saw a tyrant yet but what was a coward."

Having lost the confidence of his men and subordinate generals, many of whom (such as Leonidas Polk) actively plotted against him, Bragg gave up command to Joseph E. Johnston at his own request. He was then called to serve Davis directly in Richmond as his military adviser. When Robert E. Lee was appointed General in Chief of the Confederate armies in January 1865, Bragg went to North Carolina to serve under Joseph Johnston until his surrender.

Basil Duke said that among Confederate generals, "none other was criticized so generally and so bitterly. Some others inspired little affection and even a certain portion of enmity; but he was widely and intensely disliked. Many general officers, of less force and ability than he had, have been popular with their soldiers and those immediately under them, but if there was any such feeling for him it utterly lacked manifestation, and the very reverse was often shown. ... He was lacking in the quick, fertile, and accurate conception and broad comprehension which makes the successful strategist; he was not an able tactician. So far from inspiring, as nearly all great captains have done, confidence and love in those who followed them, General Bragg aroused sentiments the very reverse. His temper was austere and even morose, his manner was repellent, his very look and bearing suggested in others distrust of his judgement, and doubt of successful achievement."

Richard Taylor suggested that a poor digestion may have contributed much to Bragg's difficult personality: "Possessing experience in and talent for war, he was the most laborious of commanders, devoting every moment to the discharge of his duties. As a disciplinarian he far surpassed any of the senior Confederate generals; but his method and manner were harsh, and he could have won the affections of his troops only by leading them to victory. He furnished a striking illustration of the necessity of a healthy body for a sound intellect. Many years of dyspepsia had made his temper sour and petulant; and he was intolerant to a degree of neglect of duty, or what he esteemed to be such, by his officers. A striking instance of this occurred during my visit. At dinner, surrounded by his numerous staff, I inquired for one of his division commanders, a man widely known and respected, and received this answer: 'General – is an old woman, utterly worthless.' Such a declaration, privately made, would have been serious, but publicly, and certain to be repeated, it was astonishing. … It may be said of his subordinate commanders that they supported him wonderfully, in despite of his temper, though that ultimately produced dissatisfaction and wrangling. Feeble health, too, unfitted him to sustain long-continued pressure of responsibility, and he failed in the execution of his own plan."

One of Bragg's subordinates, BrigGen Arthur Manigault, was in the small minority who at least respected Bragg: "I have always regarded him as one of the best organizers of an army and disciplinarians that I ever met with, and he possessed many of the qualities essential to a commander. Full of energy, indefatigable in his labors, firm and impartial as an administrative officer, he was no respecter of person or rank, and punished a delinquent, be he the general next below him, or the meanest soldier in the ranks, the one with as little hesitation as the other. A terror to all quarter-masters and commissaries, no trains ever stopped on the way, or were out of place, and seldom was there any grumbling about the quantity or quality of food. And in like manner from the Lieutenant-general down to the company subaltern, all knew that to disobey an order or to be delinquent in any way, was sure to bring the iron hand down upon his head. I think that the army under his command, all things considered, was in a higher state of efficiency whilst he ruled than ever before or after. At first he was an exceedingly unpopular officer; all feared, none liked him, but it was not long before they found him out. Leaving out the higher grades of officers, such as held prominent commands, with whose electioneering plans for political capital and the sinister ambitious views he interfered with or exposed, he was as a general thing much more loved than any other in like position. The rank and file of the army became much attached to him, and in spite of his misfortune parted with him with regret. He was not, however, a great general; made many mistakes, some of which he was not responsible for; was always overmatched in numbers, and when pitted against Grant, his inferiority was too evident. His campaign around Chattanooga, after the victory of Chickamauga, showed great deficiency both as a tactician and strategist. The least said about it, the better for his reputation. Personally, I learned to like him, although at first much prejudiced against him; but he certainly was excited by the purist patriotism, and one of the most honest and unselfish officers of our army."

After the war Braxton Bragg worked as an engineer in Alabama and Texas, where he died on 27 September 1876. He is buried in Mobile, Alabama.

A wartime picture of Bragg, clean-shaven, as he appeared to the Southern public. The coat appears to be fastened in the 'female' direction, but the portrait, as so often, has been reversed left to right during the process of engraving from the original photograph. (*Southern Illustrated News*)

BRECKINRIDGE, John Cabell (1821–75)

John C.Breckinridge **(see Plate E2)** was born on 15 January 1821 near
Lexington, Kentucky. A graduate of Centre College (1839), he studied
law at Transylvania University and passed the bar to practice law in
Lexington in 1845. Breckinridge was a major in the 3rd Kentucky
Volunteers in the Mexican War; afterwards he used his war record to
go into politics, entering the Kentucky Legislature in 1849 and the
US House of Representatives in 1851. He became vice-president under
James Buchanan in 1856, but was actually elected to the US Senate from
Kentucky in 1859 while still holding that office. He ran for president
in 1860, but drew far fewer votes than Abraham Lincoln.

On 2 November 1861, after Kentucky joined the Confederacy, he
became a Confederate brigadier-general. John Jackman, a private in
his brigade, noted in his diary that, "He is the most eloquent speaker I
ever heard ." Breckinridge was promoted to major-general on 14 April

1862. At Shiloh that month he commanded the Reserve Corps, and later successfully commanded the defenses of Vicksburg. His attack on Baton Rouge failed, but he served well at Murfreesboro (Stones River, 31 December 1862–3 January 1863) and Chickamauga (19–20 September 1863), as well as under Joseph Johnston during the 1863 Vicksburg campaign. At Missionary Ridge (25 November 1863) he was responsible for picking a poor defensive position that was easily crushed; Bragg later claimed that the hard-drinking Breckinridge had been inebriated throughout the battle. In 1864 he was given command of the Department of Southwest Virginia, serving in the July 1864 "raid on Washington". He was named Secretary of War on 4 February 1865, too late to do much to influence the by then obvious outcome of the war, although he served competently in the post.

Basil Duke later noted that: "His ability as a statesman, his political astuteness, and extraordinary power as an orator were universally recognized and acknowledged, and it may be because of that – because he had exhibited so conspicuously the talents which make a man eminent and distinguished in civil affairs – that due credit was not given him for the talent he undoubtedly had for war. At any rate, while his reputation in the Confederate army was good, and he was ranked among the best of those who held high but subordinate rank, it was not what I think it should have been. … His courage and resolution were superb. I have never, I think, witnessed an indifference to danger so absolutely calm and imperturbable as I have seen him display under very extraordinary exposure to personal peril. His chief defect as a soldier – and, perhaps, as a civilian – was a strange indolence or apathy which at time assailed him. He illustrated in his official conduct the difference between energy and persistent industry. When thoroughly aroused he acted with tremendous vigour, as well as indomitable decision; but he needed to be spurred to action, and without some special incentive was often listless and lethargic. Nature seemed to have formed him to deal with emergencies. … I never saw a man more loath to give or take offense, or one so patient with the, perhaps, over-zealous suggestions of younger subordinates, and the occasional petulance which seems an inevitable concomitant of volunteer military service."

Breckinridge was one of those who chose to flee the country after the fall of the Confederacy, since his previous status as vice-president laid him more open than most to prosecution for treason. After a hair-raising escape to Cuba he traveled to England, and

A fine surviving example of a Confederate brigadier-general's regulation dress coat, in gray faced and edged white, with gold braid Austrian knots on the sleeves and three wreathed gold stars on the collar. This coat belonged to BrigGen James Pettigrew, who in fact served in the Eastern theater. *(Gettysburg National Military Park)*

from there to Canada, returning to Kentucky in 1869 after the Universal Amnesty. Although frequently asked to return to politics, he shunned the spotlight, practicing law until his death on 17 May 1875 in Lexington, where he is buried.

BUCKNER, Simon Bolivar (1823–1914)

Simon Bolivar Buckner (**see Plate B3**) was born in 1823 in Hart County, Kentucky, the son of a veteran of the War of 1812. He entered the US Military Academy, and was graduated eleventh in a class of 25 in 1844. He served in the Mexican War, where he was slightly wounded and twice brevetted. Thereafter he was an instructor in infantry tactics at West Point until he resigned in 1855. He moved to Chicago, where his wife had inherited valuable real estate, and entered business there. He also entered the Illinois militia, gaining the rank of major. After returning to Louisville, Kentucky, he continued his interest in the militia, forming the Kentucky State Guard (some 4,000 pro-slavery volunteers) and commanding it with the rank of brigadier-general.

Strongly pro-Confederate, Buckner declined an offer of a brigadier-general's commission in the US Army. Nevertheless, he was shocked when Polk's troops invaded neutral Kentucky; on 21 September 1861 he wrote to Jefferson Davis' government in Richmond pleading for the withdrawal of the Confederate forces, pointing out that there was no military advantage in the move and a number of political disadvantages. Even so, a day later he became a Confederate brigadier-general. Buckner was third in command at Fort Donelson in February 1862 when his superiors – John Floyd and Gideon J.Pillow – abandoned their posts and fled; he surrendered the fort to Grant, a pre-war personal friend. After exchange, Buckner commanded a division in the Army of Tennessee in the Kentucky campaign, fighting at Perryville (8 October). In December 1862 he was sent to command the defenses of Mobile, Alabama. He was given command of the Department of East Tennessee in May 1863, commanding a corps at Chickamauga (19–20 September 1863). After that he was sent to the Trans-Mississippi Department where he was named a lieutenant-general, chief of staff to E.Kirby Smith.

Buckner set great store by social poise, favoring those who demonstrated grace and style rather than rough and tactless people – something of a handicap to command in the rural West of the Confederacy. A strong opponent of Braxton Bragg, he appears to have been the author of a petition signed in October 1863 by almost all of Bragg's corps and division commanders requesting his replacement.

After the war Buckner moved to New Orleans, returning to Kentucky three years later to become editor of the *Louisville Courier*. In 1887 he was elected state governor, and ran unsuccessfully for vice-president in 1896. He died on his estate near Munfordville, Kentucky, on 8 January 1914, the last surviving Confederate to have been a major-general or above. He is buried at the State Cemetery, Frankfort, Kentucky.

CHEATHAM, Benjamin Franklin (1820–86)

Benjamin Franklin Cheatham (**see Plate F3**) was born on 20 October 1820 in Nashville, Tennessee, into a wealthy family. He served as a captain of the 1st Tennessee Volunteers in the Mexican War, and at Buena Vista (22–23 February 1847) he formed a dislike of Jefferson

OPPOSITE
A portrait of Benjamin Franklin Cheatham made from a pre-war photograph, to which a Northern photographer had added his idea of a Confederate uniform. *(Photographic History of the Civil War)*

"Old Frank" Cheatham in a wartime photograph recording a less idealized image; an eye-witness recalled his "red bulldog face and close cropped, savage moustache." Note the buttoned-back lapels, and the buttons set on in pairs, which identify his rank as brigadier-general. Cheatham had a reputation as a brave, hard-drinking, foul-mouthed officer, if not a particularly skilled commander. Nevertheless, he must have been popular with his men: some 30,000 people turned out for his funeral in Nashville in September 1886. *(Military Images Magazine)*

Davis and his 1st Mississippi Rifles for claiming glory that he felt belonged to his regiment. After the war he went to California to open the Hotel de Mexico in Stockton, handling patrons attracted by the 1849 gold rush. There he became a local political power; on one occasion he even held the town's sheriff at gunpoint to make him release a prisoner for a mob to lynch. After several years he returned to Tennessee to take up farming, and became a major-general of state militia.

When Tennessee seceded Cheatham was named a brigadier-general in the state army, and was second on the list of the same rank in the Provisional Army of Tennessee in May 1861. On 9 July 1861, he was named a Confederate brigadier-general. He was promoted major-general to rank from 10 March 1862, as a result of his part in the battle of Belmont (7 November 1861). Cheatham's service was in the Army of Tennessee, in which he commanded first a brigade and later a division. He handled his command poorly at Murfreesboro (Stones River, 31 December 1862–3 January 1863), where some said he was drunk; he was at first late to attack, and then sent his brigades in piecemeal, only redeeming himself somewhat by personally leading a charge late in the day.

Despite this, Cheatham was given command of a corps in the Army of Tennessee, dating from fall 1864 when John B.Hood took over that army. Cheatham's and Alexander Stewart's corps failed to cut the Columbia–Nashville Turnpike when the Federal armies were falling back towards Franklin in November 1864, and Hood blamed Cheatham for that failure, despite his own lack of involvement in making the move. Again it was repeated throughout the army that Cheatham had been drunk at the time, and another rumor had him spending the wasted time with a local beauty.

Cheatham was a true frontiersman, with a profane vocabulary that he did not hesitate to use. One of his soldiers described him as "one of the wildest men I ever heard speak"; and a British visitor later noted in amusement, "It is said that he does all the necessary swearing in the 1st *corps d'armée*, which General Polk's clerical character incapacitates him from performing." Despite his tongue and his fondness for the bottle, he was known as a regular church attendee; John Jackman, a Kentucky Brigade private, noted in his diary on 4 April 1864, "Nearly always see Gen'l B.F.Cheatham at church."

Private Philip Stephenson, Washington Light Artillery, recalled "Old Frank" as "the personification of your bluff, cursing, swearing trooper – a sort of Blücher. A good soldier and fighter, and as a rule reliable to execute orders, but too fond of whiskey and a brawler when drinking. A middle sized, sturdy man of middle age with a red bulldog face and close cropped, savage mustache. Easy going, fond of his men, familiar with and careful with them and they fond of him!"

Stephenson told a story of how after the battle of Belmont, Cheatham, "in liquor of course," cursed an Irish private who replied, "'Sure an if you wasn't a general, ye would not do that!' Cheatham pulled off his coat and said, 'There's the general and here's old Frank Cheatham. Come on!' and the man took him at his word! Nothing was done with him, I believe."

After the war Cheatham ran unsuccessfully for the US House of Representatives in 1872, but served as Tennessee's superintendent of state prisons. He was appointed postmaster for Nashville, dying in that post on 4 September 1886. He was buried in Mount Olivet Cemetery in that city, and his funeral was attended by some 30,000 people, including many of his old command.

CLEBURNE, Patrick Ronayne (1828–64)

Patrick Cleburne (see Plate F2) was born in Bridgepark Cottage on the River Bride, ten miles west of Cork, Ireland, on 17 March 1828. His law partner before the war and aide-de-camp during it, L.H.Mangum, later wrote: "Patrick was fond of boyish adventures, but he avoided companionship and preferred his dog, his horse, his rod or his gun to other company. Even in those early days he was noted for his high sense of honor and his keen sense of disgrace. In literary taste he was fond of history, travels, and poetry, but whether it was due to some peculiar mental inaptitude or to the disgust created within him by the pedagogue who had delt out the classics by the rule of iron, he was very deficient in Latin and Greek."

Apprenticed to an apothecary, Cleburne failed to pass the Latin and Greek examination to become one himself, and so feared this failure would bring shame on his family that he enlisted in the 41st Regiment of Foot in February 1846, believing that the regiment was shortly to be sent overseas. Within three years he became a lance-corporal and then a corporal. Later he discovered that a relative was a captain in the same regiment, although of a different company. Although this relative promised him that he would eventually be commissioned in the regiment, he decided to purchase his way out of the British Army in 1849.

Sailing thereafter for America, Cleburne took a job as a druggist's clerk in Cincinnati, Ohio, moving after six months to Helena, Arkansas. There he became part owner of a drugstore while reading law, and was admitted to the bar in 1856. A former member of the (Protestant) Church of Ireland, he became a vestryman at St John's Episcopal Church in Helena, a member of the Sons of Temperance, and of a Masonic lodge. In 1856 Cleburne and a friend, Thomas Hindman, were involved in a political debate that spun out of control when the two were attacked on the street by gunmen. Cleburne was shot in the back, but turned and returned fire, killing one of the shooters and driving the

other three into the rear of a store; there they hid until Cleburne collapsed, when they ran. Cleburne and his friend both recovered from their wounds. He also helped organize a volunteer militia company, the Yell Rifles, in 1859, and in January 1861 he participated in taking over the Little Rock Arsenal.

On the outbreak of the Civil War, Cleburne joined the Confederate Army as a private, but he was quickly elected captain and, in May 1861, colonel of the 15th (originally the 1st) Arkansas Regiment, under William Hardee's overall command. He and Hardee became close friends, and Hardee helped Cleburne learn his drill system as well as his other duties. Cleburne, called "Old Pat" by his men, was made a brigadier-general on 4 March 1862. Wounded in the face while leading a charge at Richmond, Kentucky (30 August 1862) during Bragg's and Kirby Smith's advance into that state, Cleburne returned in time to participate in the battle of Perryville on 8 October, where he was again wounded. He was made a major-general on 13 December 1862; Bragg said that Cleburne was "cool, full of resources and ever alive to success." Cleburne himself joked to a British visitor that he owed his rank "mainly to the useful lessons which he had learnt in the ranks of the British Army, and he pointed with a laugh to his general's white facings, which he said this 41st experience enabled him to keep cleaner than any other Confederate general." (The regiment had white facings.) In fact, Patrick Cleburne became the best general in the Western theater, distinguishing himself at Murfreesboro (Stones River, 31 December 1862–3 January 1863) and receiving a vote of thanks from Congress for his actions at the close of the Chattanooga campaign a year later.

On the other hand, Pte Philip Stephenson recalled that Cleburne was "as bad a judge of a horse, for he never was mounted on a decent animal. At a review on one occasion he almost upset the gravity of us all in the ranks in spite of discipline and our respect for him, by lumbering along far in the wake of the rest of the dashing cavalcade, on his clumsy old plough horse of an animal. It had stumbled and almost thrown him, and he couldn't catch up again."

Cleburne owned no slaves and, being foreign born, he had no sentimental attachment to or vested interest in the institution. He therefore easily recognized that Southern African-Americans presented an opportunity as well as a *causus belli*, and in January 1864 he proposed arming them and forming them into military units. Joseph Johnston simply told him that the idea was too political and that Cleburne should not propose it; another general at the meeting where the idea was discussed said that it was treasonable, and demanded that Cleburne put it in writing. Cleburne duly gave him a letter, which the general sent to the government in Richmond. This document was quickly covered up by shocked officials; but even holding the opinion ruined Cleburne's chances for further and deserved promotion.

Cleburne's soldiers later told the story that on the way to the ill-fated town of Franklin, Tennessee, in November 1864 the general passed a bare-footed captain limping along. "Come here and pull off my shoes," Cleburne called out to the man. He protested, but Cleburne insisted, saying, "I am on horseback and can get along better than you can." He made the officer take them and put them on, and then rode off into battle in stockinged feet on a cold, wintry day. On foot after two horses had been shot under him, Cleburne was killed near the old gin-house at Franklin by a single bullet through the heart, while leading one of many charges during Hood's impetuous and costly attack of 30 November. He is buried at Helena, Arkansas.

Basil Duke later wrote: "Gen. Patrick R. Cleburne has been sometimes termed the Stonewall Jackson of the West [a nickname Jefferson Davis gave him], and, while it cannot be claimed that he possessed the genius of Jackson, the appellation is unquestionably extremely apposite. He had the same dauntless temper and patient, unflagging energy, the same conscientious, almost fanatical devotion to duty, and an equally combative inclination as a soldier. ... I cannot remember that I ever saw an officer who was so industrious and persistent in his efforts properly to drill and instruct the men under his command. He took great interest in everything connected with tactics, and personally taught it all, and was occupied from morning until night in superintending squad, company, and battalion drill, guard mounting, inspection and, indeed, everything mentioned in the books or that he could conceive of. ... He was unlike Stonewall Jackson in one particular; when angered, annoyed or astonished, he would swear, and, although his oaths were brief, they were intensely energetic. His speech ordinarily had little of the Irish accent, and was slow, clear, and precise, but in his moments of excitement or dissent the brogue became broad and clear... .

"He was extremely temperate and simple in his mode of life, reserved and studious; and was an ardent botanist. No braver or more resolute man ever lived, but he was warm-hearted and generous to a degree and devoted in his friendships. He was skillful, I believe, in the use of all arms, but was extraordinarily so with the pistol... ."

John Bell Hood, who had few good words to say about any of his subordinates, later wrote that Cleburne "was a man of equally quick perception and strong character, and was, especially in one respect, in advance of many of our people. He possessed the boldness and the wisdom to earnestly advocate, at an early period of the war, the freedom of the negro and the enrollment of the young and able-bodied men of that race."

DUKE, Basil Wilson (1838–1916)

Basil Wilson Duke (see Plate E3) was born in Scott County, Kentucky, on 28 May 1838. After attending Centre College and Transylvania Law School, he began practicing law in St Louis, Missouri. When the crisis over the 1860 election arose, he joined a pro-Southern organization known as the "Minute Men," which he later described as "of a semi-political and military character." Armed with a motley collection of old muskets and modern handguns, the group planned to capture the arsenal in the city. As one of a small group of representatives of this group, Duke went to Montgomery, Alabama – then the Confederate capital – on 6 April 1861. He met with Jefferson Davis and the Secretary of War, obtaining an order permitting them to take the arsenal and allowing them weapons to do so. The group arranged for weapons in Louisiana and then returned to St Louis. After meeting with the pro-Southern governor, he was warned that a pro-Union grand jury in St Louis had indicted him for treason, and he was advised to leave the area.

Duke then returned to Kentucky, where he served temporarily as acting adjutant in the 2nd Arkansas Regiment and saw duty as a scout, before joining the Lexington Rifles, his brother-in-law John Hunt Morgan's company, in which he was elected first lieutenant. When

Basil Duke, standing center, with a ribbon tied to the third button of his frock coat, was photographed while a prisoner at Fort Delaware after being captured with his brother-in-law, John Hunt Morgan. This Kentucky cavalry officer left many valuable personal impressions of his fellow Confederate generals. (Photographic History of the Civil War)

the company became a part of the 2nd Kentucky Cavalry he became lieutenant-colonel, and eventually the regimental colonel. Duke later described his regiment as made up of "reckless, dare-devil youngsters, always eager for adventure and excitement, who if they had not 'charity for all', certainly bore little 'malice to none.'"

Duke was captured with Morgan in Ohio, but was exchanged, and appointed a brigadier-general on 15 September 1864; he was given command of Eastern Kentucky and Western Virginia. His brigade escorted Jefferson Davis as he fled into Georgia, being the last uniformed unit to accompany the president before his capture. After the war Duke practiced law, and went into state politics. He died in New York City on 16 September 1916, and is buried in Lexington, Kentucky.

FORREST, Nathan Bedford (1821–77)

Nathan Bedford Forrest (see Plate H2) was born in Bedford County, Tennessee, on 13 July 1821, to a poor family. Formally schooled for only six months, he was only barely literate for the rest of his life; yet by the outbreak of the Civil War he had made a large fortune as both a slave dealer and a planter. Unusually for a man from such a background, he did not drink, smoke or chew tobacco, although he did have a notoriously fierce temper, and burst into profanity when provoked.

On the outbreak of war he enlisted as a private in the 7th Tennessee Cavalry, but then paid for his own mounted battalion, of which he was elected lieutenant-colonel in October 1861. His was the only command to escape from Fort Donelson when it was surrendered to Grant in February 1862, his men following him through a cold swamp that had been left unguarded. In April 1862 he was elected colonel of the 3rd Tennessee Cavalry, and was given command of a cavalry brigade in Bragg's Army of Tennessee two months later. Although he lacked any formal military training and disdained to study professional literature, as a leader of raids in the enemy's rear Forrest showed an innate genius, and some argue that he was the greatest cavalryman that America has ever produced. He was commissioned brigadier-general on 21 July 1862 after capturing the Union garrison at Murfreesboro – Gen Thomas Crittenden's 1,200-strong brigade and an enormous quantity of stores; he then pushed on towards Nashville, burning railroad bridges and diverting two divisions from the Federal Army of the Ohio. Basil Duke later recalled that John Hunt Morgan once asked Forrest how he had done so well at Murfreesboro: "Oh," Duke quoted Forrest as saying, "I just took the short cut and got there first with the most men." In December 1862 he led 2,500 riders on a three-week raid across Grant's lines of communication in West Tennessee; and the following summer he participated in the Chattanooga campaign.

A contemporary portrait of Nathan Bedford Forrest. General Dabney Maury first saw him in April 1862: "In stature he was over six feet, with a physical development of great strength and activity. His eyes were light gray, his cheek bones were high, his hair brown and straight, his complexion generally pallid. But those who have seen him in the heat of battle can never forget the martial beauty and grandeur of the man. A bright hectic color then glowed in his cheeks and his eyes gleamed with the light of his fierce spirit, and I have heard men say, who were by him then, that nothing could surpass or eradicate the impression of his aspect." *(Photographic History of the Civil War)*

One incident will have to suffice to give an idea of his character. Unhappy with Lieutenant A.Wills Gould, one of his artillery officers, Forrest ordered the man transferred. The enraged Gould confronted Forrest at his headquarters, pulling out a pistol and firing it directly into Forrest's side. Forrest, although badly wounded, managed to grab Gould's arm with one hand, while with the other pulling out a penknife that he opened with his teeth, and stabbed the lieutenant in the stomach. Gould pulled away and ran; a hastily summoned doctor made a quick examination and told Forrest that his wound was mortal, whereupon Forrest jumped up to exclaim that no man would kill him and live. Dashing outside, he grabbed a pistol from a saddle holster and crossed the street to a tailor shop where Gould had collapsed from his wound. When the general entered the shop, Gould got up and made for the back door; Forrest followed, firing and missing, although he hit a spectator. Gould reached an empty lot where he again collapsed into the weeds. Bystanders had by then grabbed the general and convinced him that the lieutenant's wound was fatal: it was, and he died several days later, after an emotional reconciliation with the general. Forrest himself recovered after about ten days' rest.

After a raging quarrel with Bragg, Forrest asked for an independent command; Jefferson Davis promoted him to major-general on 4 December 1863 and gave him a free rein, with a command based in north Mississippi and west Tennessee. Between February and October 1864 he outwitted and outfought much larger Federal forces, earning the sobriquet of "that devil Forrest" from the frustrated Gen Sherman. He beat Gen W.Sooy Smith at Okolona on 20 February; raided into

Kentucky as far as Paducah in March, and on 12 April captured Fort Pillow, where he stained his reputation by, if not ordering, then at least ignoring his men's massacre of white Tennessee Union men and African-American soldiers. On 10 June 1864 he routed Gen Samuel D.Sturgis' much larger force at Brice's Cross Roads; and returned to the Army of Tennessee as cavalry commander after Hood replaced Johnston in July. On 14–15 July, now with 10,000 men under his command, he forced Gen A.J.Smith to withdraw from Tupelo; and on 21 August he raided Federal headquarters at Memphis, forcing Gen C.C.Washington to flee in his nightclothes. He then moved east and north and, in concert with Joseph Wheeler, harassed Sherman's lines of communication between Atlanta, Nashville and the Ohio river. In late October–November he captured US Navy vessels on the Tennessee river near Johnsonville, where he threatened a large Federal depot and bluffed the defenders into burning their own stores, while he took and destroyed 26 cannon, four gunboats, 14 transports and 20 barges. Forrest was then ordered to march eastwards to join John B.Hood in the Franklin and Nashville campaign. He was promoted to lieutenant-general, ranking from 28 February 1865; but his war ended when he was decisively beaten by the young Union cavalry general James H.Wilson at Selma, Alabama, in April 1865. During the war Forrest had been wounded four times and had 29 horses shot under him, and it was said that he killed about 30 men with his own hand.

Brigadier-General Arthur Manigault later assessed Forrest: "As a Cavalry leader … he was by far the most able and combined many qualities, such as skill, courage, judgment, and the power of organizing and disciplining troops, which would have made him conspicuous anywhere. His defective education and social disadvantages were his great drawbacks. Had he been more fortunate in these respects, he would in all probability have been the most conspicuous and useful general in the Army of the Confederate States."

Forrest returned to plantation life after the war, further tarnishing his reputation by becoming the first leader of the Klu Klux Klan. Named president of the Selma, Marion & Memphis Railroad, he died on 29 October 1877 at Memphis, where he is buried.

GARDNER, Franklin (1823–73)

Franklin Gardner (see Plate C1) was born in New York City on 29 January 1823. His family moved to Iowa, and from there he was appointed to West Point, being graduated in the class of 1843; he later earned two brevets for gallantry in the Mexican War. Gardner never officially resigned from the US Army, although he accepted a commission as lieutenant-colonel of infantry in the regular Confederate Army on 16 March 1861. He was apparently motivated wholly by personal

Franklin Gardner, born in New York and raised in Iowa, was the defender of Port Hudson on the Mississippi river during the longest siege ever conducted on American soil; he surrendered on 9 July 1863 only after the fall of Vicksburg made his own position untenable. *(Photographic History of the Civil War)*

principle; his brother served in the Union army and his father worked for the US government during the war.

Gardner actually served as commander of a cavalry brigade at Shiloh (6–7 April 1862), being named brigadier-general ranking from 11 April. He returned in an infantry brigade command in the Kentucky campaign, and was appointed major-general on 10 June 1863. He commanded the defenses of Port Hudson in 1863, sustaining the longest siege on American soil, and finally surrendering on 9 July only after he learned that Vicksburg had fallen, making his post untenable. Robert Patrick of the 4th Louisiana noted in his diary on 4 January 1863, "Major-general Gardner is in command here now and he is a very strict disciplinarian. He says that no man shall be allowed to go outside of the lines under any pretext... ." Even so, Gardner was unjustly suspected by some of Union sympathies on account of his Northern birth.

Exchanged in August 1864, he was sent to the Department of Mississippi, where he remained until the Confederate surrender, although Bragg had tried unsuccessfully to get him assigned to the Army of Tennessee as a corps commander. After the war he was a planter near Lafayette, Louisiana, where he died on 29 April 1873, and is buried.

HARDEE, William Joseph (1815–73)

William J. Hardee (see Plate C3) was born in Camden County, Georgia, on 12 October 1815; his grandfather had fought in the Revolutionary War and his father in the War of 1812. Graduating 26th in the West Point class of 1838, he was sent on to the French cavalry school at Saumur for further study. On his return he taught his regiment the tactics he had learned there, being promoted to captain. Captured with his company on the onset of the Mexican War, he was soon exchanged and given a position in Scott's army in its drive on Mexico City, receiving two brevets for gallantry.

Hardee was later appointed commandant of cadets at West Point. He was best known for his standard drill manual, *Rifle and Light Infantry Tactics*, first published in 1855, which was to some degree a translation from a contemporary French Army manual. He revised this work in 1860 to reflect the adoption of a longer rifle-musket by the US Army, although most Northern wartime editions were reprints of the original manual. In fact the linear tactics that Hardee proposed became virtually obsolete with the introduction of accurate, long range weapons, and U.S. Grant later admitted that he never actually read the manual closely.

Hardee resigned his commission on 31 January 1861, and accepted a commission as colonel commanding the 1st Georgia Infantry (Regulars) on 7 February, immediately organizing the defenses of Savannah as well as heading a board to pick the uniform and equipment of the state's forces. He was then given command of Fort Morgan on Mobile Bay by the Confederate government. With danger looming in the West, he received a Confederate brigadier-general's commission on 17 June 1861, and command of the troops in Arkansas. Hardee was promoted to major-general on 7 October 1861, and sent to the Army of Tennessee before the battle of Shiloh the following April. Private William Watson, 3rd Louisiana Infantry, expressed an enlisted man's view when he wrote that Hardee "was a bold leader and a skillful tactician. ... He was particularly noted here for making surprise attacks, skillfully planned,

upon the enemy's right wing as they advanced their works, so that when any heavy cannonading was heard on our left the remark would be, 'Oh, it is old Hardy [sic] driving back their right wing.'"

Hardee ended up as a wing commander in the Kentucky campaign and at Murfreesboro (Stones River, 31 December 1862–3 January 1863). Promoted to lieutenant-general ranking from 10 October 1862, he thereafter held a corps command. He was offered army command, but declined it, having a real dread of responsibility. He later wrote, "I am glad the responsibility does not rest with me, it is weighty and I would not bear it if I could."

Hardee's men trusted him. Private Philip Stephenson, Washington Light Artillery, later wrote: "He was 'Old Reliable,' the standing favorite of all officers, with us all. Men may come and men may go, but 'Old

Reliable' stood by us forever. That was our feeling. ... He was immovable when on the defensive, headlong like a thunderbolt when on the aggressive, always self-possessed, resourceful, daring in the midst of cautiousness, prudent in the very height of an onset, in short, an all around soldier and man. ... True, he always exacted rigid discipline, but no man was more in sympathy with his men." However, his superior Bragg fell out with him over tactics at Murfreesboro, writing to Richmond that Hardee "is a good drill master, but no more, except that he is gallant. He has no ability to organize and supply an army, and no confidence in himself when approached by an enemy."

During the 1863 campaign a British visitor noted that Hardee "is a widower, and has the character of being a great admirer of the fair sex. During the Kentucky campaign last year, he was in the habit of availing himself of the privilege of his rank and years, and insisted on kissing the wives and daughters of all the Kentuckian farmers." Hardee later met and courted the 25-year-old heiress to a wealthy Alabama planter, and married her in February 1864. After a short honeymoon, he returned to his corps command.

When John B. Hood, whom he mistrusted, took over the Army of Tennessee, he requested and was given the command of Savannah, which shocked his men. Philip Stephenson believed that "Hardee was the staff the whole army had leaned upon after Johnston left. ... In Hardee's departure was the beginning of the destruction of the Army of Tennessee." Once in Savannah Hardee set up defenses, and later successfully evacuated them on the approach of Sherman's army. Thereafter he opposed Sherman's advance through the Carolinas until his eventual surrender in April 1865. Apparently not all of his subordinates approved of Hardee. Major-General Lafayette McLaws wrote home from Savannah in October 1864, "How any one can be patriotic under the leadership of Hardee is beyond my comprehension."

At the end of the war Hardee told a reporter: "I accept this war as the providence of God. He intended that the slave should be free, and now he is free. ... I was one of the hot Southerners who shared the notion that one man of the South could whip three yankees; but the first year of the war pretty effectually knocked that nonsense out of us, and, to tell the truth, ever since that time we military men have generally seen that it was only a question of how long it would take to wear our army out and destroy it. We have seen that there was no real hope of success, except by some extraordinary accident of fortune, and we have also seen that the politicians would never give up till the army was gone. So we have fought with the knowledge that we were to be sacrificed with the results we see to-day, and none of us could tell who would live to see it."

Basil Duke later wrote: "General Hardee was a thoroughly educated and exceedingly accomplished soldier. No one in the old army, perhaps, was more perfectly versed in either the more important or the minutest details of professional knowledge. I believe that it is admitted that he had no superior as a corps commander, and his capacity for handling troops on the battle field and his skill as a tactician were unsurpassed. ... I believe that he possessed almost every quality which is necessary to make an able general, unless it may have been self-confidence. His grasp of a strategic question or situation was clear and comprehensive, and as an army leader he was prompt, bold, and alert. I have sometimes heard

General Hardee characterized as a martinet. This is not just to him. He believed in careful discipline and was sometimes strict in enforcing its essentials. But he was never harsh, and was not only solicitous for the comfort of his men, but entertained the kindest feeling for them."

After the war Hardee became a planter at Selma, Alabama, where he was buried after his death on 6 November 1873.

HILL, Daniel Harvey (1821–89)

Daniel H.Hill (see Plate C2) was born in York District, South Carolina, on 12 July 1821. He was a sickly child, and suffered all his life from a frail constitution and a chronic spinal condition. His father died when he was four, and the family of a widow and 11 children lived in poverty on a farm growing corn and cotton. Hill later remarked, "I had no youth." Appointed to West Point, he graduated 28th out of 56 cadets in the class of 1842, where one friend noted his "honor, courage, and frankness." He subsequently earned two brevets for gallantry in the Mexican War, during which he served in the 4th Artillery Regiment. On 2 November 1848 he married a North Carolina socialite; he resigned from the army on 28 February 1849, and became professor of mathematics at Washington College and Davidson College. In 1859 he was appointed superintendent, professor of mathematics and artillery, and president of the board of directors of the newly created North Carolina Military Institute.

Hill also published a mathematics textbook which was most noted for its anti-Northern bias, basing questions on such ideas as "The field of battle of Buena Vista is 6½ miles from Saltillo. Two Indiana volunteers ran away from the field of battle at the same time, one ran a half a mile an hour faster than the other, and reached Saltillo 5 minutes and $54\%_{11}$ seconds faster than the other." The book had only limited national sales. Hill, a Presbyterian elder, also published two religious studies, *A Consideration of the Sermon on the Mount* and *The Crucifixion of Christ*.

Hill was named colonel of the 1st North Carolina Infantry Regiment on its formation. Sent to the Richmond area, he commanded at the first action of note, Big Bethel (10 June 1861), and was promoted to brigadier-general on 10 July. He was appointed major-general on 26 March 1862, and served in the Army of Northern Virginia until 14 July that year, when he was given the job of negotiating a prisoner exchange. Subsequently Hill was sent to command the Department of North Carolina. Lee wrote to President Davis a short time later, "I fear General Hill is not entirely equal to his present position. An excellent executive officer, he does not appear to have much administrative ability. Left to himself he seems embarrassed and backward to act." Davis then had him returned to command of his old division in the Army of Northern Virginia. "Old DH" fought well through the 1862 Maryland invasion, although his physical health began to decline, noticeably adding to his depression thereafter.

On 1 January 1863, Hill submitted his resignation to the War Department, but he was called to Richmond and there given command of the Department of North Carolina, which included Virginia south of Richmond, to replace E.Kirby Smith. Hill and Robert E. Lee quarreled about how many and which troops Hill needed in this command. He was promoted to lieutenant-general on 11 July 1863, and given a corps

A portrait photograph and an engraving of D.H.Hill as a brigadier-general. Sickly all his life, Hill rose from a childhood of grinding rural poverty to become a published mathematician and a Presbyterian elder as well as a lieutenant-general; unsurprisingly, he was not known for a sunny disposition or a generous tolerance of his fellow officers. General Moxley Sorrel described him as "a small, delicate man, rather bent, and cursed with dyspepsia, which seemed to give color to his whole being." *(Military Images Magazine; Battles and Leaders of the Civil War)*

command in the Army of Tennessee, fighting in the Chattanooga campaign that autumn.

Always noted for his harsh criticisms of Confederate cavalry and artillery generally, as well as of his superiors and fellow generals, Hill was one of the most vocal opponents of Braxton Bragg. Bragg accused Hill of being the reason for the lack of complete success in the Chickamauga campaign: "Genl Hill is despondent, dull, slow, and tho gallant personally, is always in a state of apprehension, and upon the most flimsy pretexts makes such reports of the enemy about him, as to keep up constant apprehension, and require constant reinforcements. His open and constant croaking would demoralize any command in the world. He does not hesitate at all times and in all places to declare our cause lost." As a result Jefferson Davis refused to submit his last commission for confirmation to the Confederate senate and, on 13 October 1863, the president authorized Bragg to remove him from command. Bragg quickly took advantage of this authority, and that was largely the end of Hill's military career. He saw a little service at Petersburg beginning in May 1864; he was then sent to command the District of Georgia, and ended the war as a division commander in the Army of Tennessee in North Carolina.

Arthur Manigault noted of Hill that he "had always borne the unenviable reputation… of having his own way and doing things only as pleased him, and, were it otherwise, throwing obstacles in the way… ." General Moxley Sorrel said of him: "He seemed not to know peril and was utterly indifferent to bullets and shell, but with all these qualities was not successful. His backbone seemed a trifle weak. He would take his men into battle, fight furiously for some time and then something weakened about him. Unless there was some strong character near by… his attack would be apt to fail and his first efforts go unrewarded."

After the war he was president of the University of Arkansas and the Georgia Military and Agricultural College, dying of cancer in a relative's home in Charlotte, North Carolina, on 24 September 1889.

HOOD, John Bell (1831–79)

John Bell Hood (**see Plate F1**) was born in Owingsville, Kentucky, on 1 June 1831, the son of a wealthy doctor. When growing up he was known as a hothead who often got into fights. From West Point, where he acquired the nickname "Sam", he was graduated 45th out of 52 cadets in the class of 1853. He served in the infantry in California and Texas, and came to consider himself a citizen

of that state. When the 2nd Cavalry was formed in 1855 Hood was given a first lieutenant's commission in that crack regiment. On the outbreak of war he resigned his commission on 17 April 1861, to accept a regular Confederate Army commission as captain, commanding a company of the 1st Confederate Cavalry Regiment. Sent to Kentucky to recruit, he then went to Richmond, where he was made a major in charge of a cavalry camp of instruction.

Hood was given command of the 4th Texas Infantry on 1 October 1861. He was promoted to Texas Brigade command, ranking as a brigadier-general from 3 March 1862, for reasons that are not clear today. However, his behavior during the Peninsula campaign of spring 1862 marked him out as a fighter. Stonewall Jackson wrote the War Department on 27 September 1862 asking that Hood be promoted, and he was named major-general ranking from 10 October 1862, being given a division to command under James Longstreet.

Courageous to a fault, John Hood failed in important aspects of higher command. He never really grasped that his new job was not primarily one of personal, inspired battlefield leadership, but one of administrative and logistical care. His men were often found poorly supplied and disciplined, while he continued to fight at the head of his division. He was badly wounded in the left arm storming Devil's Den at Gettysburg on 2 July 1863; although the arm was saved there was permanent nerve damage, probably to his elbow, that cost him the use of his hand. Returning to duty, he lost his right leg at Chickamauga in September 1863; its shattered bones had to be amputated at mid-thigh. The wound was thought mortal at first, and rumors of his death abounded; however, he was brought back to Richmond where he did recover by late October. Veterans of his old Texas brigade chipped in to buy him a cork leg, and he was able to get around on it with crutches; he found that he could ride if strapped into the saddle, and his soldiers started calling him "Old Pegleg." On his return to duty he was appointed lieutenant-general on 1 February 1864, since Jefferson Davis had decided to replace D.H.Hill's name on the list with Hood's, and the latter was given a corps command.

Hood went behind Joseph Johnston's back to complain of his conduct during the Atlanta campaign. "I have done all in my power to induce General Johnston to accept the proposition you made to move forward," he wrote to Bragg – then serving as Davis' military adviser – on 13 April 1864. "He will not consent, as he desires the troops to be sent here and it is left to him as to what use should be made of them."

On 12 May 1864, Hood, who had attended St Paul's Episcopal Church in Richmond with Davis while recovering from his amputation, was baptized into that church by the Right Reverend LtGen Leonidas Polk. One of his staff officers, a Roman Catholic, was less than impressed with the ceremony: "There stood the battered old hero (barely thirty years old). There the warrior Bishop Polk. And there stood your humble servant with a flaring tallow candle in one hand and a horse-bucket of water in the other."

When Joseph Johnston was relieved, Hood was given the temporary rank of general on 18 July 1864, and command of the Army of Tennessee. Brigadier-General Arthur Manigault wrote that "Hood's exhibition of generalship whilst with the army, and up to the time of his promotion to its command, had proved him unfitted for the command of a corps, so that it is not surprising that as their leader, the army received the announcement with a very bad grace, and with no little murmuring. Shortly after assuming the command, and it became evident what his plan of

Wartime photograph of John Bell Hood, and an engraving made from it. Despite the *gravitas* lent to his appearance by the full beard, he was only in his early thirties. Stephenson of the Washington Light Artillery wrote of him: "He was over six feet and of splendid proportions. His hair and beard were of a light yellow and worn long. The eyes were large and bold, but of a singular light grey... . He usually wore an 'undress uniform,' but was always scrupulously neat and even elegant in attire." On the other hand, one of his staff officers noted that Hood was a "tall, rawboned country-looking man" who "looked like a raw backwoodsman, dressed up in an ill-fitting uniform." Here he displays the unwreathed collar stars so often worn by general officers. (*Military Images Magazine; Battles and Leaders of the Civil War*)

operations was to be, and system of attacks, it was seen that if continued, a very few more engagements would destroy the whole army, and that the lives of men were being thrown away to no purpose, he not having eye or head to take advantage of the successes which the army twice gained by its valor, which Joseph Johnston or Stonewall Jackson would have seized with avidity, and have brought about a very different result."

In a short time Hood convinced many of his men that he could be a good leader. Philip Stephenson recalled him as "easily approached, of frank, open demeanor and lenient rule, of magnificent and striking presence. … He won the hearts of all men right and left." Buckner, however, found Hood an easy target for his urbane wit, later saying that "Hood never gets out of any scrape unless he can fight out."

Disappointed in an attempt to win the hand of a flirtatious South Carolina debutante, and in constant pain from his wounds, in action Hood demonstrated little ability to command an army. He wasted his troops in fruitless attacks at Peachtree Creek (20 July), Atlanta (22 July) and Ezra Church (28 July), and finally abandoned Atlanta (31 August). He tried to lure Sherman out of the city by threatening his communications, but failed; and as Sherman headed into Georgia in mid-November, Hood marched north into Tennessee towards Nashville. His soldiers had mixed feelings about this campaign. Robert Patrick of the 4th Louisiana noted in his diary when it started, "I fear this campaign will prove a failure though I will continue to hope for the best. I have no confidence in Hood's abilities. He is a good, rough fighter, but when that is said, all is said. He hasn't the knowledge of military affairs that Johnston possesses."

Although his advance was rapid, Hood slept while he had a chance to capture retreating Federals at Spring Hill (29 November), blaming Cheatham for his own failure. The next day he attacked MajGen John M.Schofield's fortified positions at Franklin, in a series of unimaginative charges without artillery preparation – some said, in order to punish his army. At Franklin, Hood inflicted some 2,300 Federal casualties but lost about 6,300 men – among them, generals Patrick Cleburne, Hiram Granbury, S.R.Gist, John Adams, Otto Strahl and John Carter killed or mortally wounded. He also forfeited what little confidence his men had had in him; Texas Capt Samuel Foster noted in his diary after that fight, "Gen. Hood has betrayed us (The Army of Tenn). This is not the sort of fighting he promised us at Tuscumbia and Florence Ala. when we started into Tenn. This was not a 'fight with equal numbers and choice of the ground' by no means. And the wails and cries of widows and orphans made at Franklin Tenn Nov 30th 1864 will heat up the fires of the bottomless pit to burn the soul of Gen J B Hood for murdering their husbands and fathers at that place that day. It can't be called anything else but cold blooded Murder."

Hood, however, totally misread the mood of his men, later writing in his memoirs that the campaign and battle created "the improved *morale* of the Army, which had resulted from a forward movement of one hundred and eighty miles – occasioned the extraordinary gallantry and desperate fighting witnessed on that field."

General Schofield retreated to prepared works at Nashville, and Hood followed, although his men were poorly equipped, clad, and fed. George Thomas, the unflappable Union commander, bided his time under impatient pressure from Washington; and when he finally struck on 15–16 December 1864 he virtually destroyed Hood's army in what has been called the completest tactical victory of the war, and forced it into headlong retreat into Georgia. Nashville completely drained Hood; Stephenson saw him on the retreat: "One look at Hood's face and bearing was enough to show us he was not equal to the occasion. We knew we could get no help from him. He made no attempt to rally the men who were in a mob all around him, to halt them, regulate their march, or anything!" Hood requested his relief, and the request was honored in January 1865. He never commanded again, and surrendered himself at Natchez, Mississippi.

Richard Taylor noted that, "Like Ney, 'the bravest of the brave,' he was a splendid leader in battle, and as a brigade or division commander unsurpassed; but, arrived at higher rank he seems to have been impatient of control, and openly disapproved of Johnston's conduct of affairs between Dalton and Atlanta. Unwillingness to obey is often interpreted by governments into capacity for command."

After the war Hood moved to New Orleans, and in a single tragic episode he, his wife, and one of their children died of yellow fever in August 1879. He is buried in that city's Metairie Cemetery.

Part of the Confederate defenses of Atlanta, Georgia, to which Joseph Johnston withdrew in July 1864; one of Jefferson Davis' worst mistakes was to replace him as commander of the Army of Tennessee with John B.Hood, whom Grant forced to abandon the city. The photograph, by George N.Barnard, was taken near the Potter House. (US National Archives)

JOHNSTON, Albert Sidney (1803–62)

A.S.Johnston (**see Plate A1**) was born in Mason County, Kentucky, on 2 February 1803. While attending Transylvania University he became close friends with fellow student Jefferson Davis. Afterwards Johnston was appointed to the US Military Academy, where he roomed with Leonidas Polk, graduating second in the class of 1826 and serving as adjutant of the Corps of Cadets. Appointed to the 2nd Infantry Regiment, he served in several Indian campaigns before he resigned his commission to care for his wife, who was dying of tuberculosis, in April 1834. Thereafter he moved to Texas to farm, arriving in the midst of the war against the Mexican central government. He was appointed a colonel and adjutant general of the Army of Texas on 5 August 1836; promoted to brigadier-general, he was given command of the army on 31 January 1837. He later resigned this post, suffering from a wound received in a duel, and was appointed Texas' secretary of war. He resigned this post later, only to return as colonel of a Texas volunteer regiment (which saw no action) for six months during the Mexican War. After his men went home, Johnston remained with Zachary Taylor's army in northern Mexico, working closely with Jefferson Davis, then colonel of the Mississippi Rifles.

Johnston was appointed a paymaster, ranking as major, in the US Army on 31 October 1849. In 1855 Davis, then US Secretary of War, got Johnston appointed colonel of the new 2nd Dragoon Regiment, stationed in Texas. He then led a US Army expedition into Utah to pacify the Mormons, who had recently massacred a group of non-Mormon emigrants in the Mountain Meadows. Remaining in Utah for almost two years, Johnston was given command of the Department of the Pacific. He was serving in this post when war broke out, and resigned his commission on 10 April 1861. His first thought was to remain in California and return to civilian life. The firing on Fort Sumter, however, led him to join the Confederate Army. He headed off by horseback from Los Angeles, across the Mojave Desert, arriving in Richmond on 5 September.

Davis was delighted to have him, noting later, "He came and by his accession I felt strengthened, knowing a great support had thereby been added to the Confederate cause. ... I hoped and expected that I had others who would prove generals; but I knew I had one, and that was Sidney Johnston." Davis appointed him a full general and on 10 September assigned him to command essentially the whole of the Western theater except for coastal defenses. With complete trust in Johnston, Davis felt that the West was safe and turned his attention to Eastern affairs, neglecting Western requirements.

It was a huge command and had very few resources. Confederate government policy was to defend every inch of ground, and the violation

A portrait of Albert Sidney Johnston done from a pre-war photograph, "mirrored" from left to right, and featuring a vague impression of a uniform; this appeared in the 28 September 1861 issue of *Harper's Weekly*. Just three weeks previously this 58-year-old veteran of the early Indian Wars, the Texan War of Independence and the Mormon expedition had ridden into Richmond to offer his sword to the Confederacy after riding through the wilderness all the way from Los Angeles. Shortly before his death at Shiloh he was described by Philip Stephenson as "tall, straight, powerfully made, dignity yet grace in every movement, gravity and care, yet sweetness in his face. His pictures do not put him forth at all."

of Kentucky neutrality made this even more difficult. Short of men and weapons, Johnston pushed what he had forward along the front, ordering raids to keep the Federals off balance. In the meantime he concentrated his forces at Corinth, Missisippi; then turned to attack U.S.Grant's troops at Pittsburg Landing before the Army of the Ohio could come up to reinforce him. In that first day of the battle of Shiloh (6 April 1862) Johnston failed to oversee the deployments he wanted, so that his right flank, which was supposed to lead and sweep along the Tennessee river, fell behind. While supervising the front line fighting Johnston was shot in the leg; not wanting to shake morale by leaving the field wounded, he continued until he fell fainting from his horse through loss of blood, and died several hours later. He is buried in the State Cemetery at Austin, Texas.

Basil Duke later wrote: "His manner and bearing, while kind and courteous, were inexpressibly majestic, and seemed the unmistakable index of a lofty character. He exercised control and leadership without effort, and under all circumstances displayed the inborn faculty of command." Duke went on, "A general who could plan and successfully execute one such campaign [Shiloh] might surely be expected, with opportunity, to accomplish other things of like nature; and we are justified, therefore, in believing that had General Johnston lived to the close of the war his Confederate record would have been inferior to none." Richard Taylor agreed, feeling that, "With him at the helm, there would have been no Vicksburg, no Missionary Ridge, no Atlanta. His character was lofty and pure, his presence and demeanor dignified and courteous, with the simplicity of a child; and he at once inspired the respect and gained the confidence of cultivated gentleman and rugged frontiersman."

JOHNSTON, Joseph Eggleston (1807–91)

Joseph E.Johnston (see Plate B1) was born in Farmville, Virginia, on 3 February 1807, a distant relation to Patrick Henry, and son of a Revolutionary War cavalry veteran. He was graduated 13th out of 46 in the West Point class of 1829, in which Robert E.Lee – a close friend – was graduated first. He served in the Seminole and Mexican Wars, being an aide-de-camp to Gen Winfield Scott, and as the lieutenant-colonel in a light infantry regiment. He was wounded four times in the Mexican War, brevetted to the rank of colonel, and gained a reputation as a personally unlucky soldier. Scott noted that "Johnston is a great soldier, but he had an unfortunate knack of getting himself shot in nearly every engagement."

Joseph Johnston was, nevertheless, always a very cautious individual. Although he was an excellent shot, friends recalled that he never pulled the trigger when hunting unless he were absolutely sure of hitting and killing his target; hence, he rarely brought home any game. Moreover, another friend noted that Johnston "hated to be beaten, even in a game of billiards."

After the Mexican War he reverted to his permanent rank of captain of Topographical Engineers, later becoming lieutenant-colonel of the 1st Cavalry Regiment. Joseph Johnston was a US brigadier-general serving as quartermaster general when the Civil War broke out, and he resigned his commission on 22 April 1861. At the time the US Secretary of War recalled that Johnston felt that secession "was ruin in every sense of the

word, but he must go." This suggests that his head was never fully in "the cause", whatever his Virginian heart told him. He was commissioned a brigadier-general in the regular Confederate Army in May 1861 and given command in the Shenandoah Valley. He eluded Federal forces there to join Beauregard's troops at Manassas in July 1861, and allowed Beauregard, his subordinate, to continue command in that battle (First Bull Run, 21 July). He was appointed a full general to rank from 4 July, and given command of the Confederate forces in Northern Virginia.

Rank was always a problem for Joseph Johnston. He felt that since he had been a brigadier-general in the pre-war US Army, even though in a staff position rather than a line command, he should have been the senior general in the Confederate Army. However, Jefferson Davis felt

1: General Albert Sidney Johnston　　　2: General Pierre Beauregard　　　3: Major-General Sterling Price

A

B

1: General Joseph E.Johnston   2: Major-General Earl Van Dorn   3: Lieutenant-General Simon B.Buckner

1: Major-General Franklin Gardner   **2: Lieutenant-General D.H.Hill**   **3: Lieutenant-General William Hardee**

C

D 1: Major-General Braxton Bragg   2: Brigadier-General John Hunt Morgan   3: Lieutenant-General Leonidas Polk

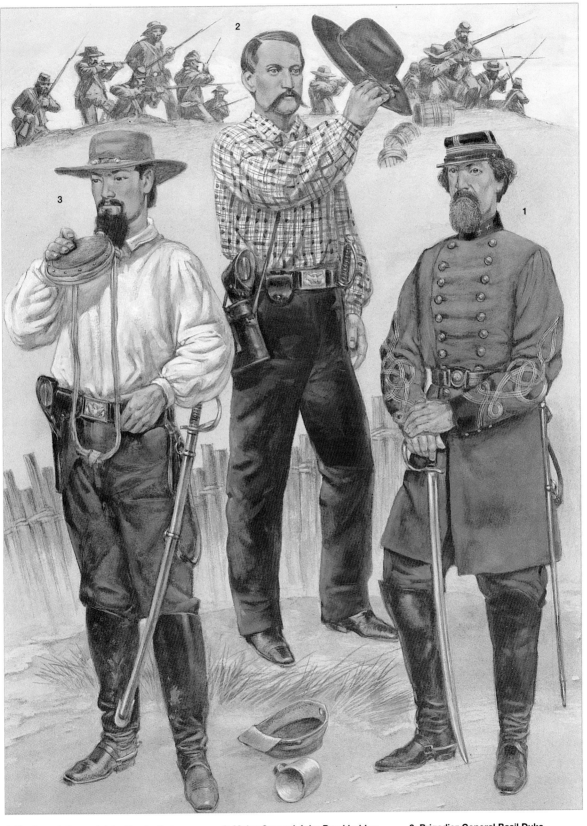

1: Lieutenant-General John Pemberton   2: Major-General John Breckinridge   3: Brigadier-General Basil Duke

F   1: General John Bell Hood   2: Major-General Patrick Cleburne   3: Major-General Benjamin Cheatham

1: Major-General John B.Magruder   2: Lieutenant-General Edmund Kirby Smith   3: Lieutenant-General Richard Taylor   **G**

H   1: Lieutenant-General Alexander Stewart   2: Lieutenant-General Nathan Bedford Forrest   3: Major-General Joseph Wheeler

that Johnston's substantive line rank was still a lieutenant-colonel in the pre-war army, and hence placed him fourth among the generals on the regular Confederate Army list. Johnston and Davis got into a letter-writing battle over this disagreement, which not only took their minds off more important tasks but caused a real rift between the two. Davis was also greatly irritated when Johnston retreated from his position around the old First Manassas battlefield: first, because Davis could see no need for it; second, because Johnston did not inform him prior to the move; and third, because Johnston pulled back so quickly that he destroyed tons of precious matériel that was both difficult for the Confederacy to replace and bound to be much needed for future operations.

Joseph Johnston's men also found him to be a strict disciplinarian. First Sergeant W.H. Andrews, 1st Georgia Regulars, recalled that "Gen.Johnston is death on drinking and the soldiers say he can smell it 400 yards with the wind against him."

When McClellan's Federal army landed on the Peninsula in April 1862, Johnston moved his troops to defend Richmond, but fell back to a point where the enemy could see the city's church steeples, again giving up precious supplies in the process. Davis so feared that Johnston would simply give up the city that he wrote him, "If you will not give battle, I will appoint someone to command who will." Johnston, his pride stung, then turned and struck at McClellan's left in the indecisive battle of Seven Pines (Fair Oaks, 31 May–1 June), in which he was once again wounded. During his recuperation he was replaced by Robert E.Lee, and when he reported as fit for duty on 12 November 1862 he was sent to command the Department of the West.

A British visitor to his headquarters there noted that, "He lives very plainly, and at present his only cooking utensils consisted of an old coffeepot and frying pan – both very inferior articles. There was only one fork (one prong deficient) between himself and staff, and this was handed to me ceremoniously as the 'guest.'"

Major-General Lafayette McLaws, who served under Johnston on the Peninsula, wrote home on 25 April 1862: "General Johnston will never speak on official matters but to the person interested, dislikes to have a crowd about him, never mentions military matters away from his office. Often rides off alone, never will have more than two with him. Has not much to say to even his best friends, and does not appear to care about dress, although he always dresses neatly & in a uniform coat – if you have business with him it is yes or no, without talking more than a proper understanding of the subject."

E.P. Alexander, who also served with Johnston on the Peninsula, was most impressed by the general's physical strength. He recalled how once "while undressing we got to talking of sabre exercises. Gen.J. partially undressed & with arms & chest nearly bare took a sabre & gave us some illustrations, & though I have seen many much more powerful cavalrymen like Gen. Hampton, Aleck Haskell, Col.Von Borcke, &c., yet I've never seen a sabre whistle & sing like that one."

A portrait of Joseph E. Johnston done from a pre-war photograph; this engraving appeared in the 5 October 1861 issue of *Harper's Weekly*. Johnston was so sensitive about his baldness that he almost always wore a hat, even at the dinner table.

Johnston performed in a lackluster manner during the siege of Vicksburg, in which his opening a line into the city was the only Confederate hope. Nevertheless, after Bragg was relieved following Missionary Ridge (second day of Chattanooga, 25 November 1863), Johnston was given command of the Army of Tennessee. The departure of that unpopular commander ensured him at least an open minded reception from its officers, and he rebuilt the army's morale by personally inspecting every unit in it, and making sure the men were finally well fed and clad.

Johnston then conducted a skillful series of fairly bloodless delaying maneuvers against Sherman while retreating on Atlanta in May–July 1864. Even these constant retreats did not sap his men's morale; Philip Stephenson recalled, "Our faith was pinned to Johnston. Our confidence in him was unbounded and we felt that if he said, 'turn and fight,' the conditions were all right and the victory was sure." On average he held Sherman's advance to a rate of about one mile a day for two-and-a-half months; but when Johnston ended up inside the city's defenses, Jefferson Davis, who wanted a more aggressive defense against Sherman, replaced him with Hood on 17 July.

Arthur Manigault thought that, "The removal of General Johnston from the command of the Army of Tennessee was one of those hasty and ill-judged steps on the part of Mr.Davis, which, I believe, contributed

The site of Joseph Johnston's surrender of the Army of Tennessee, as well as Confederate forces in the Carolinas, to Gen William T.Sherman in April 1865. *(Photographic History of the Civil War)*

materially to the downfall of the Confederacy, and possibly it caused it. I have always thought that had General Johnston been permitted to retain the command, Sherman never would have gained Atlanta."

All ranks felt the same way, putting their utmost faith in Johnston. "Gen.Johnson [sic] has so endeared himself to his soldiers, that no man can take his place," the Texan Capt Samuel Foster noted in his diary on hearing that Hood was replacing him. "We have never made a fight under him that we did not get the best of it. And the whole army has become so attached to him, and to put such implicit faith in him, that whenever he said for us to fight at any particular place, we were in feeling like Gen Johnson knew all about it and we were certain to whip. He never deceived us once. It is true we have had hard fighting and hard marching, but we always had something to eat, and in bad weather, or after an extra hard march we would have a little whiskey issued. He was always looking after our comfort and safety. He would investigate our breastworks in person, make suggestions as to any little addition or improvement that would make them safer or more comfortable. Gen Johnson could not have issued an order that these men would not have undertaken to accomplish – For the first time, we hear men openly talk about going home by tens (10) and by fifties (50). They refuse to stand guard, or do any other camp duty, and talk open rebellion against all Military authority – All over camp, (not only among Texas troops) can be seen this demoralization – and at all hours in the afternoon can be heard Hurrah of John Johnson and God D—n Jeff Davis."

The 4th Louisiana clerk Robert Patrick noted in his diary on 12 May 1864, "I consider Gen. Johnston the best General in the Confederacy, not even excepting Robt. E.Lee... ."

Despite President Davis's feelings about Johnston, Lee brought him back to command armies in the Carolinas when trying to stop Sherman's drive north though those states in February 1865. It was too late to change the outcome of the war by this point, and Johnston told Davis this when the president passed by his forces fleeing from Richmond. Davis gave Johnston permission to negotiate a surrender, which he did on 26 April 1865.

Secretary of the Navy Steven Mallory later wrote: "The Confederate armies included many educated and efficient men in high grades, gentlemen of Christian faith and practice, and of military genius, experience, and capacity; but, in the judgment of those who served under him, there was none who could be more truthfully designated as a soldier *sans peur et sans reproche* than 'Old Joe." When Gen James Longstreet was later asked who was the best Confederate general, he replied, "I am inclined to think that General Joe Johnston was the ablest and most accomplished man that the Confederate armies produced. He never had the opportunity accorded to many others, but he showed wonderful power as a tactician and a commander. I do not think that we had his equal for handling an army and conducting a campaign."

After the war Johnston was elected to the US House of Representatives, before being named the US Commissioner of Railroads. Marching bareheaded in the funeral procession of William T.Sherman, Johnston caught cold which developed into pneumonia, and died on 21 March 1891. He is buried in Green Mount Cemetery, Baltimore.

John Bankhead Magruder – "Prince John" – poses here in an elaborate version of Confederate full dress, with a number of personal affectations such as epaulettes, aiguillettes and a laced pouch belt in the European style. His later commission as a major-general in the service of the Mexican Emperor Maximilian no doubt gave him even more scope for indulging his dandified tastes. (Author's collection)

MAGRUDER, John Bankhead (1807–71)

John B.Magruder (**see Plate G1**) was born in Port Royal, Virginia, on 1 May 1807. He was graduated in the West Point class of 1830, and the following year he married a Maryland lady with whom he had three children. He received three brevets for gallantry in the Mexican War, where he served in the artillery. Stationed later along the Canadian border, he lived up to his nickname of "Prince John" : when asked the cost of some item that he served as part of a formal dinner that he hosted for visiting British officers, he turned to his servant and said, "Cost? I have no idea. How much was this, after all?"

He resigned his captain's commission on 20 April 1861, and received a Confederate brigadier-general's commission on 17 June. He was promoted to major-general on 7 October, and was in command on the Peninsula when McClellan's Federal army landed there in April 1862 for a drive on Richmond. Digging in along old British trench lines at Yorktown, Magruder bluffed the Federals by making a large show of bringing in train after train of the same men looking like reinforcements. McClellan dug in for a formal siege, but before they could open it Magruder, now under Joseph Johnston's direct command, retreated on Richmond.

His troops held part of the Confederate capital's defenses when Robert E.Lee, the new commander there, attacked in the Seven Days' Battles (26 June–2 July 1862). Major-General McLaws, who served with Magruder on the Peninsula, wrote home on 25 April that "General Magruder is fond of dress and parade and of company. Conceals nothing, and delights to have a crowd about him, to whom he converses freely upon any and all subjects. He never moves from his head quarters without having five or six aides & a dozen or more orderlies… General Magruder can talk twenty four hours incessantly."

Lee was unimpressed by what he judged as Magruder's lack of aggressive behavior, and had "Prince John" reassigned to command the District of Texas, New Mexico, and Arizona. There he recaptured the important Texas port of Galveston, and held off the Federals.

After the Confederate surrender, Magruder joined the forces of the French puppet emperor of Mexico, the Austrian Archduke Maximilian, and was commissioned a major-general in his service. When Juarez's forces finally defeated the foreign interventionist troops and their imperial allies, Magruder returned to the US to make his home in Houston, Texas. He died there on 18 February 1871, in genteel poverty, and is buried in Galveston.

MORGAN, John Hunt (1825–64)

John Hunt Morgan (**see Plate D2**) was born in Huntsville, Alabama, on 1 June 1825. Educated at Transylvania College, he enlisted for a year's service as first lieutenant in the 1st Kentucky Mounted Volunteers in the Mexican War, and saw action at Buena Vista. After mustering out in 1847 he failed in an attempt to secure a regular US Army commission, and moved to Lexington, where he worked as a businessman and, at one point, as a slave dealer. He organized a local volunteer militia company, the Lexington Rifles, in 1857, and gained a local reputation as a serious gambler. Morgan's first wife died in 1861, just before he enlisted his company into Confederate service.

When the war broke out Hunt took his company to Bowling Green, Kentucky, to join Simon Buckner's state forces, and was named colonel of the 2nd Kentucky Cavalry on 4 April 1862. An effective leader, he was promoted brigadier-general on 11 December that year. Thereafter he was noted for carrying out a series of raids towards the Ohio and Indiana borders, which earned him a vote of thanks from the Confederate Congress. Morgan took time off from his duties on 14 December 1862 to marry 21-year-old Martha Ready.

Morgan realized the value of the telegraph before many of his contemporaries; he recruited a telegraph operator who accompanied the unit during their raids, so that from time to time he could tap into a line and intercept Union messages, giving the command intelligence on the location of enemy pursuit parties. The group would also capture telegraph stations, and Hunt's operator would go on line impersonating the station operator to feed false information to the Federals. As Basil Duke recalled, "He would sometimes on such occasions compel the captured operator to telegraph at his dictation, meanwhile observing very carefully the man's manner of working the instrument. Then having apparently caught his style or 'handwriting,' he would take the instrument himself."

Morgan's fame grew when Sally Ford, a popular novelist, published *Raids and Romance of Morgan and His Men* in Mobile, Alabama, in 1863; the novel was banned as seditious in Memphis and St Louis.

Morgan and his band were captured near New Lisbon, Ohio, on 26 July 1863, and he was locked up with several of his officers in the Ohio State Penitentiary. The group managed to tunnel their way out, however, escaping on 27 November and returning to Southern lines. Thereafter Morgan was given command of the Department of Southwestern Virginia in April 1864. In this command, while bivouacked at Greenville, Tennessee, on 3 September 1864, he was attacked by a detachment of Federal cavalry. Trying to escape, he was shot down and killed in the garden of the house in which he had been sleeping. He is buried in Lexington, Kentucky.

Brigadier-General John Hunt Morgan in the uniform he apparently wore for his wedding (see Plate D). Again, note the style of wearing the coat with only the top pair of buttons fastened. Although heavily retouched this is in fact a photograph. (*Photographic History of the Civil War*)

ABOVE LEFT **A woodcut engraving of John Hunt Morgan in the full dress uniform worn at his wedding in December 1862. This Alabama-born leader of Kentucky cavalry raiders was killed in September 1864, one of 77 of the 425 Confederate general officers to die or suffer mortal wounds in battle; another 19 died of other causes. Considering that many of the total never held field commands, the actual proportion of killed among those who saw combat must have been at least one in four. (Battles and Leaders of the Civil War)**

PEMBERTON, John Clifford (1814–81)

John C.Pemberton **(see Plate E1)** was born in Philadelphia, Pennsylvania, on 10 August 1814, and was graduated 27th out of 50 graduates of West Point's class of 1837. In the Mexican War he was brevetted to captain for gallantry, as well as receiving a presentation sword from the citizens of Philadelphia and a vote of commendation from the Pennsylvania legislature. Ulysses S.Grant recalled that in Mexico it was ordered that junior officers were not allowed to ride on horses during marches, but most officers received verbal permission to ride since walking in the rough terrain was difficult for officers used to riding. Pemberton, however, "would walk, as the order was still extant not to ride, and he did walk, though suffering intensely the while. ... He was scrupulously particular in matters of honor and integrity."

Although Northern born, Pemberton was always pro-Southern and a strong supporter of states' rights. Richard Taylor recalled meeting Pemberton, then a young US Artillery officer, on the Canadian border in the mid-1840s, and being surprised by the strength of his opinion on states' rights, "unusual among military men at the period." This feeling was encouraged when he married Martha Thompson, a native Virginian, in 1846.

When the Civil War broke out, Pemberton resigned from the US Army on 24 April 1861 to offer his services to Virginia, which commissioned him a lieutenant-colonel in the state's army. He was named a brigadier-general on 17 June; and in November he was appointed to the same rank in the Confederate Army and given command of the Department of South Carolina, Georgia, and Florida. He was promoted to major-general to rank from 14 January 1862, after Lee left to go to Western Virginia. However, the Northern-born Pemberton's brusque and reserved manner did not sit well with the touchy, hot-headed local South Carolina officials. The governor himself wrote Jefferson Davis saying that Pemberton was "confused and uncertain about everything," and asking for his removal.

Beauregard was brought in to replace Pemberton, who was assigned to command the Department of Mississippi and Eastern Louisiana and, after Van Dorn's defeat at Corinth (3–4 October 1862), he was promoted to lieutenant-general to rank from 10 October. As such, the defense of Vicksburg, the last major stronghold on the Mississippi, fell on his shoulders. On 25–29 December 1862 he fought off Gen Sherman's attacks at Chickasaw Bluffs north of Vicksburg. Probing and naval operations continued during the winter, but by the end of April 1863 Gen Grant was ready to close in, fighting his brilliant three-week campaign on the Big Black River. Joseph Johnston, the overall theater commander, was driven out of Jackson, Miss, by much stronger Federal forces on 14 May, and after an action at Champion's Hill on the 16th, Pemberton was forced to withdraw within the Vicksburg defences with 30,000 men on 19 May. Johnston advised that the city be abandoned, but President Davis wanted it held. While Gen Sherman maneuvered to prevent any relief attempt by Johnston, Grant besieged Vicksburg, bombarding it from land batteries and river vessels. On 4 July 1863 – a day which Pemberton picked in the mistaken hope that it would make Grant generous over the terms – Pemberton surrendered his hungry fortress.

After Pemberton's surrender there was much talk in the South of his Yankee birth, and claims that he had joined the cause only to betray it. Richard Taylor pointed out that this was unlikely: "Certainly he must have been actuated by principle alone; for he had everything to gain by remaining on the Northern side." Even so, after his exchange Pemberton was generally distrusted, and no place requiring a lieutenant-general could be found for him. He resigned that commission in 1864 to revert to the rank of lieutenant-colonel of artillery, serving as an artillery inspector in Virginia until the end of the war. Afterwards he farmed near Warrenton, Virginia. Still later he returned to Pennsylvania; he died at Penllyn on 13 July 1881, and is buried in Philadelphia's Laurel Hill Cemetery.

POLK, Leonidas (1806–64)

Leonidas Polk (**see Plate D3**) was born into a wealthy plantation family in Raleigh, North Carolina, on 10 April 1806. After attending the University of North Carolina he entered the US Military Academy class of 1827, where he became friends with fellow cadet Jefferson Davis. There Polk was greatly affected by Chaplain Charles McIlvaine, converting to the Episcopal faith, and after a year's military service Polk resigned to enter a seminary; he was ordained in 1830. Eight years later he was called as missionary bishop of the Southwest, an area including Alabama, Mississippi, Louisiana, Arkansas, Texas, and the Indian Territory. He bought land in Louisiana, which served as his main economic support, and traveled widely establishing churches. As the diocese grew too large for one bishop, he was named Bishop of

Louisiana in 1841. A run of bad luck caused him to lose his land, and he moved to New Orleans.

At the outbreak of the Civil War he decided to offer his military training to the Confederacy. His old friend Jefferson Davis quickly commissioned him a major-general from 25 June 1861, although he had virtually no military experience and should more properly have been given, at best, a field grade in a line regiment first. However, he was promoted to lieutenant-general ranking from 10 October 1862, and organized the Army of Mississippi, which later became part of the Army of Tennessee. On the plus side, Polk knew the people and land of the Mississippi Valley, which he was given to defend. However, he soon made an error in violating Kentucky neutrality in the fall of 1861 by moving troops into Columbus, Kentucky. At first he was ordered to withdraw, but the Richmond government then changed its mind, despite an order from the state legislature on 12 September calling on the Confederates to leave.

Replaced as theater commander by Albert Sidney Johnston, Polk was given a corps, which he led at Shiloh, Perryville and Murfreesboro in 1862, at Chickamauga in 1863, and in the early Atlanta campaign of 1864. Bragg reported that Polk was one of the causes of the failure of the Chickamauga campaign, noting that he was "gallant and patriotic," but "luxurious in his habits," adding, "He has proved an injury to us on every field where I have been associated with him." As a friend of President Davis, however, Polk was safe from any criticism, and was retained in his command.

Leonidas Polk, from a (reversed) woodcut that appeared in *Harper's Weekly* on 25 October 1862. A fellow priest and friend described him: "Of good stature and an erect military carriage, broad shouldered and deep in the chest, with a well-poised, shapely head, strong but finely-cut features, one white lock overhanging his wide forehead, clear complexion, and keen but frank and kindly blue eyes, the first glance recognized him as a man to be obeyed; a closer scrutiny revealed him as a man whom noble men might love, and meaner men might fear."

The site of Polk's death in action near Marietta, Georgia. (*Photographic History of the Civil War*)

Here a photographer has painted a Union general's uniform onto an earlier photograph of Polk. Philip Stephenson described him as being "a man of most noble presence, six feet in height, well proportioned, straight, soldierly, and dignified in bearing, clear cut, handsome features, clean shaven, except little tufts of grey side whiskers. His straight broad brow was overhung on one side by one lock of his thick wavy silvery hair." *(Photographic History of the Civil War)*

During the early Atlanta campaign, at Pine Mountain, near Marietta, Georgia, on 14 June 1864, he was reconnoitering Federal positions with Joseph Johnston and William Hardee when a Federal cannon opened fire on the group, killing Polk instantly. Philip Stephenson, an eyewitness, recalled that one shot passed by; then "a second shot came, struck Polk in the left arm, tore through his heart, and through his body. It then struck a tree and exploded."

A fellow priest and friend felt that Polk was little acquainted with the classics and only knew American canon law. Still, "In conversation he was wonderfully charming. In preaching and writing he was clear and vigorous, but at times diffuse. His habit of mind was to grasp at the root-principles of things, and the clearness of his thoughts was always apparent, though his style of composition lacked the graceful facility of expression, the fertility of illustration, and the facility of arrangement which belong to the accomplished scholar."

Polk was described by one of his aides, Henry Watterson: "Wrapped in his old gray hunting-shirt, with slouched hat and sabre, he sat on his horse and received the leaden compliments of the enemy with complacent yet not indifferent good humor. … In battle he was a daring old man… He was kind and considerate of his own men; he was approachable and self-denying in his own person; and he did not know the name of fear. … He was every inch a gentleman, without mannerism or assumption – simple and innocent, yet dignified and imposing."

Polk was first buried in Augusta, Georgia, but his remains were later re-interred in Christ Church Cathedral, New Orleans.

PRICE, Sterling (1809–67)

Sterling Price (**see Plate A3**) was born in Prince Edward County, Virginia, on 20 September 1809, the son of a moderately wealthy planter. He was graduated from Hampden-Sydney College, later studying the law. He moved to Chariton County, Missouri, to practice law in 1831, and also went into business as a merchant and tobacco planter. He saw service in a campaign that drove the Mormons out of Missouri. Going into politics, he served in the state legislature and US Congress, quitting to serve as colonel of the 2nd Missouri Volunteers in the Mexican War. He was commissioned brigadier-general of volunteers during that war, and served as military governor of New Mexico. This was unfortunate, since he was a poor administrator; his neglect caused the inhabitants to rise in a revolt which he led his troops to suppress. He also led them into the Mexican province of Chihuahua, against War Department instructions. His lack of ability to follow orders would be demonstrated again during his Confederate service.

Leaving the Army after the war, Price returned home to serve as governor of Missouri from 1853 to 1857. He opposed secession,

This engraving of Sterling Price from the 12 October 1861 issue of *Harper's Weekly* shows him in the uniform of a US Army brigadier-general; in fact he had held this rank in the Missouri Volunteers during the Mexican War, before returning to politics. Personally likeable despite his vanity and blustering, and careful of his men, "Old Papa" had limited talents as a general, which were exposed during his attempted invasion of Missouri in spring 1864.

although he endorsed a resolution calling for secession if Kansas were admitted to the Union as a free state. He also opposed the pro-Union force that put down the pro-Southern Missouri forces, and ended up in command of the pro-Southern state militia after the war broke out. Price was praised by fellow Southerners as having "native good sense" rather than professional military training. On the other hand Jefferson Davis, who considered Price "the vainest man he had ever met," believed in West Point training, so the two were bound to clash.

Price fought for the Southern cause at Wilson's Creek (10 August 1861) and later captured Lexington, Missouri. However, he was forced to retreat into Arkansas, where he served at Elkhorn Tavern (7 March 1862) under Earl Van Dorn. Although that battle was a Confederate failure, Price, known as "Old Pap" or "Old Papa Price," was commissioned a Confederate major-general ranking from 6 March 1862. Private William Watson, 3rd Louisiana Infantry, thought he was "zealous, plodding, cautious, and exceedingly careful and attentive to the wants of his men, and was very popular."

Price went to Richmond in April 1862 to discuss the possibility of being transferred with his troops to Arkansas. In a stormy meeting during which this request was denied, Price shouted "Well, Mr President, if you will not let me serve you, I will nevertheless serve my country. You cannot prevent me from doing that. I will send you my resignation, and go back to Missouri and raise another army there without your assistance, and fight under the flag of Missouri, and win new victories for the South in spite of the Government."

Davis quickly replied, "Your resignation will be promptly accepted, General; and if you go back to Missouri and raise another army, and win victories for the South, or do any service at all, no one will be more pleased than myself, or more surprised." "Then I will surprise you, sir!" Price snapped back.

Price quickly submitted his resignation; but Davis had cooled down and realized Price's political importance in Missouri. He refused the resignation, writing Bragg to allow Price's Missourians to go back to the west bank of the Mississippi when possible. Thereafter Price commanded an independent force dedicated to retaking Missouri. He failed, however, at Iuka and Corinth in October 1862 and at Helena, Arkansas, in July 1863. He was successful in defense during the Camden expedition in 1864; but his final drive to liberate Missouri in September–October that year failed when he was unable to penetrate Federal defenses around St Louis. Defeated at Westport (23 October 1864), he was forced to retire into Texas.

After Price's disastrous raid into Missouri in 1864, Trans-Mississippi commanding general E.Kirby Smith wrote to Jefferson Davis: "Genl Price's name and popularity would be a strong element of success in an advance on Missouri, but he is neither capable of organizing, disciplining nor operating an army, he should not be left in command of the District [or] of an Army in the field." His soldiers agreed: Pte Watson later wrote that Price's "masterpiece in military tactics was retreating... ." One of his staff officers believed that he had "the roar of a lion but the spring of a guinea pig."

On a personal level, however, Basil Duke wrote that "it is impossible for any one who knew him personally to mention his name without some tribute to his exceeding kindness of heart and grandeur of character. He impressed all who approached him with the conviction that he was a good, as well as a great, man."

When the last Confederates surrendered, Price fled into Mexico to join Maximilian's cause. With the victory of the Juaristas he returned to Missouri in 1866, dying in St Louis on 29 September 1867. He is buried in that city's Bellefontaine Cemetery.

An engraving made from a wartime portrait of Price. Note the embroidery completely enclosing the three stars on his collar. Franklin Gardner's surviving coat has the same, rather than the regulation wreath, and Earl Van Dorn was photographed with the same style of insignia. It may therefore have been standard in the Western theater. *(Battles and Leaders of the Civil War)*

SMITH, Edmund Kirby (1824–93)

E.Kirby Smith **(see Plate G2)** was born on 16 May 1824 at St Augustine, Florida. His family planned a military career for him and, after an early education at Benjamin Hallowell's Preparatory School in Virginia, they got him into West Point, from where he was graduated in the class of 1845. However, he had narrowly escaped expulsion for demerits and, after graduation, was almost denied a commission because of poor eyesight. He was assigned to the infantry, and served in the Mexican War, earning brevets to captain for gallantry at Cerro Gordo (18 April 1847) and Contreras (20 August 1847). Smith returned to the Academy as professor of mathematics from 1849 until 1852, when he was sent west for the Indian Wars.

When the Civil War broke out Smith was a major of cavalry. He refused to surrender Fort Colorado to Texas militia; but despite this

Major-General Edmund Kirby Smith, who was promoted to that rank in October 1861 after First Manassas, where he had made a decisive intervention and had been wounded. His later career did not vindicate the high opinion which he formed of himself as a result of this episode. *(Military Images Magazine)*

demonstration of loyalty, he resigned his commission on the secession of his home state. He then joined the regular Confederate Army as the lieutenant-colonel, 1st Confederate Cavalry Regiment, in Texas in April 1861. Going to Virginia, he served in the Shenandoah Valley as a brigadier-general, ranking from 17 June 1861. On 21 July he brought his brigade into battle at the right moment to sway the tide of First Manassas (Bull Run), and survived a bullet wound in the chest. The fame Smith gained from this episode of lucky timing went to his head, and he began to see himself as a military genius; he was unwilling to take orders with which he disagreed or to co-operate with others.

Recovering by September 1861, he married a Virginia girl on the 24th of that month. For his gallantry he was promoted major-general on 11 October 1861 and, after a honeymoon, he was assigned to command the Department of East Tennessee. Smith served in Bragg's summer 1862 Kentucky invasion, winning an important action against an outnumbered Federal force at Richmond, Kentucky, on 30 August. On 9 October 1862 he was appointed a lieutenant-general, and was sent to command the Trans-Mississippi Department. After the fall of Vicksburg in July 1863, Smith became essentially the military ruler of the area, with only intermittent ties to the Richmond government. To recognize the importance of this role he was commissioned a full general on 19 February 1864.

When it became obvious that the war was lost, Smith fled to Mexico, leaving his subordinates to actually surrender his forces on 26 May 1865. After the defeat of Maxmilian's regime he returned to serve as president of the Pacific and Atlantic Telegraph Company. Later he was appointed president of the Western Military Academy in Nashville, and subsequently, chancellor of the University of Nashville. From 1875 until his death he was professor of mathematics at the University of the South, founded by Leonidas Polk as an Episcopal college. Edmund Kirby Smith died at Swanee, Tennessee, on 28 March 1893, and is buried there.

STEWART, Alexander Peter (1821–1908)

Alexander P.Stewart (**see Plate H1**) was born in Rogersville, Tennessee, on 2 October 1821. He was graduated 12th out of 56 in the West Point class of 1842; and after short service in the artillery, he was called back to the Academy to teach mathematics. He resigned his commission only three years later to become professor of mathematics and natural and experimental philosophy at Cumberland University, moving later to Nashville University. During his time there Stewart, a devout Presbyterian, organized one of the first chapters of the Young Men's Christian Association.

Stewart disapproved of slavery but believed in a state's right to secede, although he voted against the secession of Tennessee. On the outbreak of the Civil War he set up camps of instruction for the Army of Tennessee, having been named a major in the artillery of the state forces to rank from 17 May 1861. In August 1861 he was given command of Stewart's Tennessee Heavy Artillery Battalion, which was posted at Columbus, Kentucky. In November he was ordered to report, without his battalion, to Albert Sidney Johnston's headquarters in Bowling Green, Kentucky; and on 8 November 1861 he was commissioned a Confederate Army brigadier-general and given a command in Polk's Corps. Fighting well, and earning the nickname "Old Straight" from his men, Stewart was promoted to major-general ranking from 2 June 1863. On 23 June 1864 he succeeded to command of the corps after Polk's death, and was promoted to lieutenant-general. In this appointment and rank he fought until the Army of Tennessee surrendered in North Carolina.

A rare wartime photograph of the imperturbable Alexander Stewart as a major-general; in June 1864 he would be promoted lieutenant-general and given command of Polk's corps on the latter's death in action. *(Photographic History of the Civil War)*

Private Philip Stephenson later wrote: "Although never regarded by the men as having qualities of greatness, we yet felt that he was a man growing before our eyes. He never seemed to make a mistake! Painstaking, obedient of orders, cool and courageous, that was Stewart. As a man he was dignified but considerate of his men, and we liked him, gave him both our esteem and confidence. His high Christian character commanded our respect. His greatest peculiarity as a soldier was, perhaps, his imperturbable temper. Nothing could startle Stewart. In battle, and defeat especially, this trait became heroism. By no sign did he ever give evidence of excitement, uneasiness, confusion, anxiety. To look at his calm tranquil face in a time of peril or doubt was to get inspiration, regain confidence and courage."

After the war Stewart returned to teach at Cumberland University before leaving to go into business in St Louis in 1870. He was named chancellor of the University of Mississippi in 1874. He resigned that post in 1886 and died in Biloxi, Mississippi, on 30 August 1908. He is buried in St Louis.

TAYLOR, Richard (1826–79)

Richard Taylor **(see Plate G3)** was born near Louisville, Kentucky, on 27 January 1826, the son of Mexican War commander and US President Zachary Taylor. He was sent to Europe for an education, returning to be graduated from Yale University in 1845. He saw military service as his father's secretary during the Mexican War, but took up life as a sugar planter in Louisiana after the war. Entering politics, he served in the state legislature from 1856 until the outbreak of the Civil War.

Despite his lack of military training, Taylor was appointed colonel of the 9th Louisiana Infantry when the war started. Sent to Virginia, he was promoted brigadier-general commanding the Louisiana Brigade under Stonewall Jackson on 21 October 1861. Taylor was complimented for the march discipline in his brigade, and was promoted to major-general on 28 July 1862. He was then sent to command the District of West Louisiana, part of the Trans-Mississippi Department. There he led the troops that repelled the Federals under Gen Nathaniel Banks in the Red River Campaign of March–May 1864, defeating them at Sabine Cross Roads (8 April). However, his commander E. Kirby Smith would not let Taylor follow up on that success, and he asked to be relieved or sent to another command.

His request was honored, and he was assigned to command the Department of Alabama and Mississippi, being promoted to lieutenant-general to rank from 8 April 1864. In May 1865 he surrendered the last uniformed body of troops east of the Mississippi River. Taylor died in New York City on 12 April 1879, and is buried in Metairie Cemetery, New Orleans.

This engraving of Alexander Stewart was made from an earlier photograph, probably after the war. A prominent scholar and active Christian, "Old Straight" lived to be 86 years old. *(Battles and Leaders of the Civil War)*

A post-war photograph of Richard Taylor in civilian dress. The victor in the Red River campaign of 1864, he was the son of Zachary Taylor, the Mexican War commander and 12th President of the United States. Like Basil Duke, he left historians valuable personal memories of his fellow officers. *(Military Images Magazine)*

VAN DORN, Earl (1820–63)

Earl Van Dorn (**see Plate B2**) was born near Port Gibson, Mississippi, on 17 September 1820; his father was a judge and his great-uncle was President Andrew Jackson. Sent to West Point after an early education in Baltimore, Maryland, he was almost expelled for demerits, but was graduated 52nd of 56 in the class of 1842 (two places above James Longstreet). Soon after graduation he was married to a 16-year-old Alabama girl, but the family insisted that she remain at home while he was off on duty, and the two spent relatively little time together. Even after the Mexican War, when he returned home after being wounded and brevetted captain, he found domestic life a bore, writing "everything is so silent. I feel too much the passing wing of time… . " Van Dorn joined

his unit on the frontier, where he was wounded three more times during the Indian Wars of the 1850s.

On the outbreak of the Civil War he resigned his cavalry major's commission and became senior brigadier-general of Mississippi State Forces, in which role he worked closely with their commander, Jefferson Davis. He assumed command of state forces when Davis became president, and passed into the regular Confederate Army as the colonel of the "paper" 2nd Confederate Infantry Regiment, although he was transferred to the 1st Confederate Cavalry regiment on 20 April 1861. A reputation for being "a splendid horseman, an enviable fist-fighter, and a good shot with a six-gun" preceded him.

On 5 June 1861, Van Dorn was promoted to brigadier-general in the provisional army. His first service was in Texas, taking the surrenders of several US Army posts there. He was then sent to Virginia as a major-general ranking from 19 September 1861, but was soon transferred to command of the Trans-Mississippi region. There he was badly beaten by Gen Samuel R.Curtis' smaller Federal force at Elkhorn Tavern (Pea Ridge, 7–8 March 1862) during an offensive into northwest Arkansas. Thereafter Van Dorn was ordered to bring his men to Corinth, Mississippi,

Earl Van Dorn, the rash and flamboyant Mississipian whose appetite for female company was his undoing. One of his soldiers described him later: "He looked to me more like a dandy than a general of an army. He was small, curly or kinky headed, exquisitely dressed, [and] was riding a beautiful bay horse, evidently groomed with as much care as his rider, who was small looking and frenchy." According to a description of 1862, "his features were regular, his forehead rather high, eyes black and fiery; lips thin and compressed, the chin was large and the jaw-bone prominent." (Battles and Leaders of the Civil War)

to join the force which Joseph Johnston was concentrating there. After the battle of Shiloh (6–7 April) Gen Beauregard retreated from Corinth in May 1862; Van Dorn and Sterling Price attacked Grant there on 3–4 October 1862, but were beaten. Although his troops escaped envelopment through the laxity of Gen Rosecrans, Van Dorn was replaced in command by John Pemberton.

The local public were pleased by Van Dorn's removal: not only had he failed to win victories, but he had imposed martial law, much against local wishes. In addition to this his personal life was considered scandalous. He was generally known as a rake as well as an excellent poker player; he was, moreover, hot tempered. When a newspaper story appeared to glorify Nathan Bedford Forrest at Van Dorn's expense, he accused Forrest of "treachery and falsehood" and drew his sword to fight right then and there. Forrest started to draw as well, but then thrust his blade back in the scabbard, saying, "General Van Dorn, you know I'm not afraid of you, but I will not fight you." Such a fight, he said, would be a bad example to the men. Despite these flaws, Van Dorn received command of Pemberton's cavalry. He was sent to raid Grant's supply lines to the north during his advance on Vicksburg in late 1862, and succeeded in capturing the stores depot at Holly Springs on 20 December.

On 7 May 1863, Earl Van Dorn was shot in the back of the head at his headquarters in Spring Hill, Tennessee, by Dr George B.Peters, a locally prominent doctor, real-estate speculator and slave trader, who claimed that the general had "violated the sanctity of his home." Van Dorn's weakness for the ladies, which had trapped him into his early marriage, had finally been the death of him; it was generally known that the general had often called on the young and pretty Mrs Peters when her older husband was absent. Peters was later tried for murder, but acquitted. Van Dorn is buried in Port Gibson, Mississippi.

Private William Watson, 3rd Louisiana Infantry, later felt that Van Dorn "would have done well to command a brigade of cavalry or a flying column of mounted infantry, but he was too rash and thoughtless to have charge of an army."

WHEELER, Joseph (1836–1900)

Joseph Wheeler (**see Plate H3**) was born in Augusta, Georgia, on 10 September 1836. He was graduated in the West Point class of 1859, and assigned to the Mounted Rifles. Resigning his commission on

Major-General Joseph Wheeler had his coat front cut in an unusual arc, as also seen in Braxton Bragg's surviving coat. Despite the *gravitas* of this portrait, and the ageing effect of the heavy beard, this daring leader of cavalry raiders, wounded three times during the war, was less than 30 years old when it ended. Recalled to US Army service for the Spanish–American War, his service in Cuba in 1898 alongside such officers as John J.Pershing was a remarkable instance of military continuity bridging the generations. (*Military Images Magazine*)

22 April 1861, he received a commission as a Confederate first lieutenant of artillery. On 4 September 1861 the 25-year-old Wheeler was named colonel of the 19th Alabama Infantry, fighting with that unit at Shiloh in April 1862. He then transferred to the cavalry, becoming chief of cavalry of the Army of Mississippi on 13 July 1862; he was promoted brigadier-general on 30 October, and major-general ranking from 20 January 1863, while still well short of his 27th birthday.

Always active, Wheeler was wounded three times and had 16 horses shot under him. His raids into the enemy rear areas were dramatic, but made little impact on the outcome of the Western campaign. When the Army of Tennessee reached South Carolina he was replaced as the army's cavalry chief by Wade Hampton. Wheeler was captured in Georgia in May 1865, and sent to a prisoner of war camp at Fort Delaware, Delaware. Released on 8 June that year, he went to New Orleans, moving a short time later to Wheeler, Alabama. He was elected to Congress in 1881; and was called back to US Army service at the age of 62 in 1898, being named a brigadier-general and commander of cavalry in the Cuban campaign during the Spanish–American War. He retired as a brigadier-general in the regular US Army on 10 September 1900. Joseph Wheeler died in Brooklyn, New York, on 25 January 1906, and is buried in Arlington National Cemetery.

Typical scene of destruction on a stretch of railroad after a cavalry raid, such as those led by Nathan Bedford Forrest, John Hunt Morgan and Joseph Wheeler. The torn-up tracks have been piled on the timber ties; when these were set alight, the heat destroyed the temper of the iron rails. (US National Archives)

THE PLATES: WEST

A1: General Albert Sidney Johnston
A2: General Pierre Beauregard
A3: Major-General Sterling Price

Private Philip Stephenson saw A.S.Johnston **(A1)** at Corinth in 1862, and later described him: "A martial figure, although dressed in citizen's clothes, the black broad cloth suit so common for gentlemen those days – tall, straight, powerfully made, dignity yet grace in every movement, gravity and care, yet sweetness in his face. His pictures do not put him forth at all. A black felt 'slouch' hat shaded his features, especially because he walked head down as though buried in deep thought." Confederate generals often started the war either in their old US Army uniforms or in civilian clothes, since it took some months before a regulation Confederate uniform could be designed, and some further time before tailors could learn the specifications and produce such uniforms.

Beauregard's elaborate uniform **(A2)** is taken from the original; the red cap was apparently his own idea. He has just received the straw hat which he holds, with three stars indicating general officer's rank – he wore it when off duty. Beauregard was quite concerned with military dress and made such additions as he felt improved the look of the uniform.

Sterling Price **(A3)** was noted as being tall and massively built. He was known for his vanity, and Pte William Watson

A post-war portrait of Joseph E.Johnston. Federal staff officer George Nichols, who saw Johnston when he surrendered in 1865, wrote that he was "a man of medium height and striking appearance. He was dressed in a neat, gray uniform, which harmonized gracefully with a full beard and mustache of silvery whiteness, partly concealing a genial and generous mouth, that must have become habituated to a kindly smile. His eyes, dark brown in color, varied in expression – now intense and sparkling, and then soft with tenderness, or twinkling with humor. The nose was Roman, and the forehead full and prominent. The general cast of the features gave an expression of goodness and manliness, mingling a fine nature with the decision and energy of a capable soldier." *(Military Images Magazine)*

this was the first regulation Confederate uniform, and often retouched it onto images of other Confederate generals, such as T.J.(Stonewall) Jackson, which they then sold to the public.

C1: Major-General Franklin Gardner
C2: Lieutenant-General D.H.Hill
C3: Lieutenant-General William Hardee

Franklin Gardner's coat, now in the Museum of the Confederacy, had separate metal stars applied within an embroidered yellow wool wreath, and less than regulation lace on the cuffs (**C1**). The insignia, although not exactly according to regulations, appears to have been common: Earl Van Dorn, among several other Western theater Confederate generals, was photographed in a uniform coat with exactly the same metal stars and yarn wreath on his collar. This variation was probably the production of a specific tailor patronised by these generals, quite likely in Mobile, Alabama. The buttons on Gardner's coat were Louisiana state issue, although the coat itself, which he wore while commanding at Port Hudson, was made by this Mobile tailor.

D.H.Hill (**C2**) was a stickler for discipline and regulations, and is illustrated wearing a largely regulation Confederate general's dress. He would have brought his uniform from the Northern Virginia area when he was sent to his North Carolina command, and hence it would reflect Eastern theater preferences rather than the Western styles he would have seen later in the war.

Private Philip Stephenson wrote of William Hardee (**C3**) that "in the latter part of the war he used to wear a brown jeans hunting suit." Jeans cloth, a mixture of cotton and wool threads, was cheaper to produce in a South that did not have a large sheep population, so much wool had to be imported. Moreover, jeans cloth is cooler and more comfortable in summer than pure wool. At least one Western Confederate general had a regulation uniform made of jeans cloth, including his vest.

D1: Major-General Braxton Bragg
D2: Brigadier-General John Hunt Morgan
D3: Lieutenant-General Leonidas Polk

On 14 December 1862, John Hunt Morgan was married to Tennessee belle Martha Ready in the biggest social event of the Western theater. Leonidas Polk (**D3**) was the celebrant at the ceremony and wore his bishop's rochet (a white, shoulder to toe vestment with wide sleeves, the fluted cuffs gathered at the wrists with black silk bands) under his

of his command described him in 1862 as "dressed in the full uniform of a general, with a cocked hat and feathers." He here wears the regulation Confederate general's uniform with buff (in practice, white) facings, four rows of gold lace in the sleeve knots, and three stars within a wreath on each side of the collar. The dark blue trousers have gold side stripes down the leg. The *chapeau bras* (Pte Watson's "cocked hat") was officially worn for dress occasions by generals and staff department officers, but very few were actually ordered or worn by Southern officers.

B1: General Joseph E.Johnston
B2: Major-General Earl Van Dorn
B3: Lieutenant-General Simon B.Buckner

Joseph Johnston is shown in the regulation Confederate general's uniform which he habitually wore (**B1**). Often, however, he simply wore three gold stars without a wreath on each collar, a departure from regulation that was so widely seen (Robert E.Lee did the same) that it was obviously an accepted practice, even though it officially identified the wearer as a colonel.

When Van Dorn (**B2**) arrived at Price's army in 1862 he was described as wearing "a blue uniform coat, a cap of the same color, embroidered with gold lace, dark pants, and heavy cavalry boots." This was probably his old US Army uniform, with a gold-laced Confederate officer's cap added as the only indication that he had changed sides.

Simon Buckner (**B3**) wears a frock coat of his own design (the original is in the Museum of the Confederacy, as is the cap shown here), which Gen Polk admired as being comfortable-looking as well as positively rebellious in appearance. Buckner was quite interested in military finery; he had designed a gray uniform trimmed with black for his pre-war Kentucky State Guard. As he was photographed in that uniform, many Northern photographers thought that

chimere (a long, black, sleeveless vest-like gown), as shown here. Polk brought his vestments with him in his camp luggage and celebrated at services such as baptisms a number of times during his military service.

Braxton Bragg **(D1)**, shown here in his surviving original coat now in the Museum of the Confederacy, was present at the ceremony, as were William Hardee, Benjamin Cheatham and all the headquarters staff of the Army of Tennessee. The generals and staff officers were all noted as wearing their best; two regimental bands supplied the music for the formal dinner and dance that followed the ceremony, which took place at a private home. Bragg was photographed wearing this coat and the regulation dark blue trousers with twin gold lace stripes down each leg. Morgan's coat **(D2)** also survives to this day, as does a photograph of him with his young bride at about the time of the marriage, in which he is wearing this coat, cap, and trousers.

E1: Lieutenant-General John Pemberton
E2: Major-General John Breckinridge
E3: Brigadier-General Basil Duke

John Pemberton is shown in the dress of a lieutenant-colonel of artillery **(E1)**, which was his substantive rank in the regular Confederate Army, and the one he held after his surrender of Vicksburg. The uniform was essentially the same as the general officer's save for the three, instead of four rows of gold lace used on the kepi and the coat sleeve knots, and the artillery's red facings. The Confederate Army lacked an ordnance corps, and artillery officers were assigned to that duty. Regulation trousers were blue, but by 1863 gray were much more common. In fact it was then that army officials asked buying agents in Europe to buy gray instead of blue trousers for the army, since gray looked better.

Perhaps because John Breckinridge **(E2)** did not come from a regular US Army background, he was obviously not especially interested in wearing regulation military dress in the field. Private John Jackman, from his brigade, noted seeing Breckinridge on 22 May 1863: "He was dressed in citizen suit, with a broad rimmed felt hat on." Basil Duke noted that Breckinridge wore "a big slouched Southern hat, with a gold cord around it… ." In action he preferred a dark blue "Kentucky jeans" uniform coat or, in warmer weather, what he called a "battle shirt" made by his wife from blue checked material.

Basil Duke **(E3)** was described as wearing blue jeans trousers, a white linen shirt, and a dusty, wide-brimmed hat when he was captured in Ohio in 1863, and such would be a typical mounted raider's garb in the field. Duke was later photographed in prison in Delaware in a regulation coat, but that was apparently sent to him there. The boots are, however, something he would have worn on a raid.

F1: General John Bell Hood
F2: Major-General Patrick Cleburne
F3: Major-General Benjamin Cheatham

John Bell Hood is shown wearing his custom-made overcoat over his dress coat; both items are today in the collection of the Museum of the Confederacy **(F1)**. There was no such thing as a regulation Confederate Army greatcoat, and indeed the army's quartermasters found themselves hard pressed to supply greatcoats at all, since they took up so much precious material. Most officers and some men had greatcoats made at home or by local tailors to their own specifications, such as this example worn by Hood. The coat he wears under the greatcoat is essentially regulation, save that it is all gray, with a narrow white piping under the gold Austrian knot on each sleeve; the rank stars were embroidered on a white oval patch and then sewn to the gray collar. It has nine buttons down each row, placed in threes to indicate a major-general's rank. Hood was photographed in a variety of uniforms, including a single-breasted sack coat with a laydown collar, and his wreathed stars insignia sewn on a lapel such as worn here by General Cleburne.

The day Patrick Cleburne **(F2)** was killed at Franklin he was described by an eyewitness as having a military cap, and "a new gray uniform, the coat of the sack or blouse pattern." This informal style of coat, also worn by Union generals, was highly popular as a comfortable field dress. Cleburne was also wearing a white shirt and vest when he was killed. His swordbelt, with its rare Arkansas belt plate, survives in the Museum of the Confederacy.

Benjamin Cheatham **(F3)** wears a standard variation on Confederate general's uniform, with the lapels buttoned back to expose the vest. In the sweltering heat of a Southern summer this was a much cooler way to wear the coat than buttoned over the front, placing two layers of cloth over the wearer's chest.

G1: Major-General John B.Magruder
G2: Lieutenant-General Edmund Kirby Smith
G3: Lieutenant-General Richard Taylor

"Prince John" Magruder is shown in an elaborate version of a dress uniform, apparently blue **(G1)**, which is taken from an early war period photograph reproduced elsewhere in this book. In the photograph he also wears a personally acquired pouch belt and aiguillettes, but though always a fop he was unlikely to wear these in the field. His fancy kepi, with the added badge in front, was custom-made for him in France.

E.Kirby Smith **(G2)** wears a plain all-gray version of the Confederate general's coat, in which he was photographed. The broad brimmed hat was much preferred over the regulation cap in the Western theater. Such hats, which became associated in the popular mind with the American "Wild West" in later years, were comfortable and provided more protection from both sun and rain.

Richard Taylor **(G3)** is shown as he would have appeared at a parade or review, in a simplified version of the regulation dress with the easier-to-obtain and more popular gray trousers

John Pemberton, in the light-colored civilian suit standing in front of the chair, formally surrenders Vicksburg to Gen Ulysses S.Grant – whose hands are typically thrust into his pockets; the meeting took place at the Stone House within the Confederate defenses on 4 July 1863. Pemberton's officers wear full Confederate uniform. This drawing appeared in the 8 August 1863 issue of *Frank Leslie's Illustrated Newspaper*.

A wartime portrait photograph of Richard Taylor. In a popular style of the day he wears his coat with the standing collar folded down and the lapels opened. *(Military Images Magazine)*

instead of dark blue. Although Taylor saw service in the Mexican War on his father's staff, he was not a professional soldier by training and hence less concerned with niceties of uniform than many other Confederate generals.

H1: Lieutenant-General Alexander Stewart
H2: Lieutenant-General Nathan Bedford Forrest
H3: Major-General Joseph Wheeler

Alexander Stewart is shown with his frock coat open at the throat to expose his black tie and white shirt **(H1)**; this was a common way to wear the frock coat, especially in undress situations. When a soldier wore a waist-length jacket or even a sack coat he generally fastened the throat button and left the rest unbuttoned.

In May 1863 one Southerner saw Forrest **(H2)** wearing "an old slouch hat and plain, well-worn gray coat and pants...." Philip Stephenson saw Forrest in 1864 "in full uniform, faded but complete, except the head gear. He wore a home made bell-crowned, low, black, beaver hat, wide brimmed. Not very pretty. In fact it could not be becoming to anybody, especially as the nap or fur was on it. It was thick though and warm...." Forrest was habitually armed with a 0.36in Colt Navy revolver that he used with deadly effect during his raids, along with a version of the US M1860 light cavalry saber; he also had revolvers holstered to his saddle.

Young Joseph Wheeler **(H3)** wears a version of the regulation dress coat; his original coat is now in the Museum of the Confederacy. This style of frontal cut is also noted on Braxton Bragg's coat; while stylish, it must have been impractical, since it would not allow the wearer to button it back easily. Wheeler, as befits a cavalry officer, also carries a cavalry saber rather than a general's and staff officer's regulation sword.

INDEX